The Nation Killers

The
Nation Killers

THE SOVIET DEPORTATION OF NATIONALITIES

Robert Conquest

MACMILLAN

© R. Conquest 1970

First published 1970 *by*
MACMILLAN AND CO LTD
Little Essex Street London WC2
and also at Bombay Calcutta and Madras
Macmillan South Africa (Publishers) Pty Ltd Johannesburg
The Macmillan Company of Australia Pty Ltd Melbourne
The Macmillan Company of Canada Ltd Toronto
St Martin's Press Inc New York
Gill and Macmillan Ltd Dublin

Library of Congress Catalog card no. 75–120344

Printed in Great Britain by
ROBERT MACLEHOSE AND CO. LTD
The University Press, Glasgow

In Memory
R.F.W.C.
1891–1959

This book, while containing much new material, is based
in the main on the author's study,
The Soviet Deportation of Nationalities,
published in 1960 and now out of print.

CONTENTS

LIST OF MAPS

INTRODUCTION

THE deportation from their homelands of eight entire nations – men, women and children – was one of Stalin's most extraordinary acts, even in that brutal and horrible period.

In this book, we trace the circumstances of the actual deportations; the removal of these nations from the list of admitted entities with the rewriting of history and geography to exclude mention of their existence; the beginnings of their rehabilitation twelve years later; the restoration of five of them to their former homes; and the long-drawn-out and only partial rehabilitation of the other three, ending with the struggle, still in progress, for their right to their own ancestral territory.

The fate of these nationalities was, of course, no accidental vagary. It was rather a test case, a declaration of overriding intent, of the view taken by the new type of state, not merely of hostile political ideas but actually of hostile cultures or races. It was part and parcel of an entire attitude to the rights of small nations under Communist Party rule, of which the basic principle had been established in Lenin's time and earlier. In Chapters 8 and 9 we consider the whole question of communist nationality policy in this light.

· · · · ·

On the southern borderlands of Russia proper lie a number of mainly Asian peoples, most of whom formerly occupied much larger territories. The ones who suffered deportation can be considered in three groups as far as the history of their annexation to Moscow was concerned.

First there are the Volga Germans, who were brought into

9

the territory as favoured immigrants by the Russian authorities themselves.

Second are the Kalmyks, inhabiting the steppe south-west of Astrakhan, who came fairly completely under Russian influence as early as the end of the seventeenth century.

And third, the Mohammedan nations of the Crimea and the Caucasus, territories which the Russians invaded only at the end of the eighteenth century, and did not finally subdue until the latter half of the nineteenth. The Crimea was annexed only in 1783, at the time of the British annexation of Oudh, and by similar methods. The Caucasian annexations were only completed in the 1860s at the time of the British annexations in Africa. In fact, these territories are not old Russian lands, or even old dependencies, but were annexed as part of the great wave of European imperialist expansion.

A comparison may indeed be made between the present situation of those parts of Asia similarly and simultaneously brought under the rule of Britain and Russia. The present map shows, instead of a vast stretch of dependent territory from the Persian Gulf to the China Sea, a few islands and strips of coast still coming under London's control. The area under Moscow's control remains the same as in Tsarist times. The Soviet argument, indeed, is that the Caucasian and other territories involved enjoy complete autonomy and are voluntarily united with Russia. This thesis is examined in Chapter 9.

These nations were deported in 1941 (the Volga Germans) and in 1943–4. The Volga Germans were in a way a special case, as were the Meskhetians. The other six were a majority of the small peoples reached, or nearly reached, by the German invasion. This fact lends force to Walter Kolarz's statement, in his *Russia and Her Colonies*, that:

> The liquidation of the republics was a warning to all other non-Russian peoples, many of whom might have found themselves in the same position had their loyalty to Russia been put to the same test as that of the Volga Germans, Crimean Tartars, and Kalmyks. Had the USSR been invaded by Japan, the Autonomous Republics of the Yakuts

and Buryato-Mongols might have suffered the fate of the Crimean and Kalmyk Republics; had it been Turkey, a similar doom might have been the lot of the Azerbaidzhani Turks.

The two main Asian minority groups of the communist empires were involved: the Muslim Turki and the Buddhist Mongol. *All* the Turkic and Mongol nations reached by the Germans were deported – in addition to others such as the Chechens who belonged to neither group.

The story of these unfortunate peoples illustrates not only the Soviet national policy but a good deal else in Soviet practices. It shows events taking place in the Soviet Union of which information could be prevented, or largely prevented, from reaching the outside world. It shows how in the Soviet Union itself facts of considerable importance can simply never be published anywhere if official policy so decides. (It is even the case that one quite important deportation – that of the 200,000 Meskhetians – remained unknown in the West until 1968, and, as far as any detail went, until 1969.) It shows the size of deportation operations which (now admittedly) have been undertaken by the Soviet authorities. It casts a considerable light on police methods in general in the USSR. It gives a clear example of how history can be rewritten. And the fact that certain Soviet claims about the prosperity and general content-ment of sections of the population are shown to have been entirely false is relevant to the validity of Soviet claims in general. On a minor point, in this connection, the validity of the quasi-unanimous votes cast in Soviet elections may be checked by the fact that the deported nations joined in these demonstrations in the same proportion as their fellows. And, to conclude, it also seems not unreasonable to judge the adequacy of official Soviet literary products by the fact that these peoples had been equipped with 'literatures' of adulation for Stalin and other party-line matter.

Nothing here matches the horror of the Nazi gas chambers. These nations were not physically annihilated. Deported with heavy casualties, their remnants scattered in distant and alien territory, their names deleted from the lists, their languages ceasing to be taught or printed, they were destined to a more gradual oblivion. Moreover, for their persecutors, the destruction of a particular nationality was not a matter of dogma, but only of political tactics. When circumstances changed, they were ready to make partial restitution.

From the point of view of the historian – even of the historian of the Stalin epoch – the story of his treatment of these small peoples may seem no more than an episode. Probably little over half a million people died as a result of it.* Yet it is an episode so startling, and so symptomatic, that it deserves the attention of all who wish a complete grasp of the system and the attitudes then established in the USSR. And this grasp, it need hardly be said, seems really essential for anyone wishing to understand the history of our times, and hence our present world.

Meanwhile, the issue is once again a living one. The demand of the Crimean Tatars in particular for the right to return to their ancient settlements in the Crimea is a major theme of the general 'liberal' opposition in Moscow; and both Russians and Tatars are even now being jailed for it.

.   .   .   .   .

My thanks are due to Mr Peter Reddaway for much help and discussion.

R. C.

---

* It was only in 1967 that the first (unofficial) Soviet figures were given of deaths suffered in the deportations. These, on the Crimean Tatars alone, were 46 per cent, 'mainly children and old people'. (Academician Andrei Sakharov, *Thoughts on Progress, Peaceful Co-existence and Intellectual Freedom*, and see pp. 160–3.)

I

THE RUSSIANS MOVE SOUTH

THE nations whose fates we are following lived for the most part towards the southern edge of the traditional Russian sphere. We usually think of the Middle East as a Mohammedan-Asian territory bounded on the north by the Soviet frontier and the Black and Caspian Seas. But the regions to the north of this boundary are as much Asian – and largely Mohammedan – as those to the south.*

Russia's expansion into the whole area is very recent. The first Russian kingdom arose in what is now the Ukraine, but was destroyed in the Middle Ages by the Mongols. The new Russia which came into being round Moscow expanded in three directions: northwards, where it absorbed and largely Russianized the Finnish tribes inhabiting what is now North Russia; eastwards through the comparatively empty stretches of Siberia, reaching the Pacific in the seventeenth century; and, much more slowly, southwards into the area where great Mohammedan and Buddhist states were already established.

From the thirteenth century, the open plains of southern and eastern Russia, including the Crimea, were occupied by the Tatar Khanate of the Golden Horde, and the Russian princes ruling the forest belt to the north were the Khan's tributaries and nominees. When the Horde disintegrated in the fifteenth century and Russia won her independence, one of the successor states was the Khanate of the Crimea. From the 1470s this came

---

* It may be noted incidentally that while it is now common in Britain and elsewhere to regard the watershed of the Caucasus as marking the frontier of Europe, the Russian preference is still to take the line of the Kuma-Manych Depression as the physical boundary between the continents.

under the suzerainty of the Turks – co-religionists of the same stock.

The Khanate held at various times a wide area, from Moldavia to the Caucasus; even in its last days of independence it covered large stretches of the southern Ukraine and of the Kuban. The Crimea itself, its stronghold and centre, is a remarkable region. Cut off from the mainland by the shallow Sea of Azov, the even shallower Putrid Sea and the Bay of Karkinit, it is an island but for a strip of sand (the Arabat) on the eastern side, and the narrow Isthmus of Perekop on the west. Most of the country is a high steppe, but towards the southern coast stands a range of mountains up to 5,000 feet high, the Yaila Dagh, separating the inland area from a coastal strip which is present-day Russia's Riviera. In this fruitful area the Tatars became famous, as they still are, for their skills as gardeners, vine-growers and fruit-farmers – as well as leather-, wool- and metal-workers. The country has always had close links with the main civilizations of Europe: in ancient times, the Greeks had settlements here, and it formed part of the Byzantine Empire. In the later Middle Ages, Genoa held the main ports, and strongly influenced the Tatars towards Mediterranean culture. Later, Greeks again came to the area, under Turkish rule, and continued this seaborne contact from the south.

The Crimean Tatars remained a barrier to Russian expansion for three centuries. As late as 1571 they captured and sacked Moscow. Their Khanate represents, in Russian literature, much of the grandeur of Oriental civilization at the time of its greatest confidence and strength. In Pushkin's *Fountain of Bakhchisarai*, the Khan Girei and his great palace are re-created for the imagination of Europe.

For many years, the area that is now the Ukraine was a practically empty buffer zone between the Khans and the Tsars. The frontier was gradually pushed south by settlements of Cossacks, and of foreign adventurers like those who temporarily formed the principality called 'Great Serbia'. And it was not until the early years of the eighteenth century that Peter the Great managed to annex Azov, on the Sea of Azov, thus for the first time reaching the southern waters. In 1711, however, he and his army suffered disaster on the Pruth, and he was forced to retrocede the town. Russia did not obtain a final foothold even on the Sea of Azov until 1739.

But as Russia grew stronger and Turkey weakened, the Crimean position became less and less secure. The crucial war came in 1763. At first Turkish ineptness was compensated for by the energy and skill of the Tatar Khan Krim Girei. He successfully invaded southern Russia, and even won the support of the Cossacks. But he died after this campaign, and the Turks were badly defeated, finally giving up their suzerainty over the Crimea by the Treaty of Kutchuk-Kainardji in 1774.

Full Russian annexation of the Crimea was preceded by the imposition in 1776 of a puppet, Khan Chagin Girei. This provoked a national rebellion in the following year, which was put down by Russian troops at the beginning of 1778. The puppet Khan was again expelled by a rebellion in 1782. And in 1783, after Chagin Girei had again been restored by Russian arms, he was forced to abdicate and the country was annexed to Russia.

The Crimea had provided a secure Tatar base for normal warfare against the enemy to the north, but once its fastnesses were penetrated, after a few years' guerrilla fighting, there was little opportunity for prolonged resistance such as occurred in the vast mountain intricacies of the Caucasus. Though the Tatars showed every sign of hostile intent towards the Russian colonizers, their occasional risings were comparatively easily mastered. They expressed their views by large-scale emigration to Turkey, especially after the Crimean War.

In the Caucasian direction, Russian expansion was at first more rapid. The collapse of the Astrakhan Khanate in 1556 left what we now call a power vacuum in the area between that city and the northern Caucasus. Over this area the Khans of the Crimea, the Persians and the Khans of Astrakhan had long maintained rival claims to suzerainty. Russia now stood as the successor state to Astrakhan.

Two local political formations dominated the north-east Caucasus. One was a sort of federation – 'the Princes of Kabarda' – to the west. The other, the principality of Tarki, headed by its Shevkal, lay in the north of Daghestan. As soon as Astrakhan fell, Ivan the Terrible decided on the foundation of the Fort Terka at the mouth of the Terek, and in 1560 a Russian force attacked the Shevkal, in support of the Kabardines. In 1561 Ivan married the daughter of Temriuk, a Kabarda prince. From that time on the Russians continually claimed that the Kabardines had submitted to their rule. A Russian document of a century later lists the princes of the family that the Russians imagined ruled over Kabarda as monarchs, whereas actually they were simply the leading princes of a loose federation. In almost every case it runs as follows: 'Prince Mastriuk; the Tsar gave him the principality of Kabarda, but in Kabarda the principality was not given to him.'

In 1593–4 a Russian force was defeated by the Shevkal. In 1604–5 the Russians were again defeated and had to abandon their advanced forts. For the rest of the century there was no forward movement.

In the 1720s Peter the Great decided to conquer the Caspian provinces of Persia. The member of his council who advised him on this forward policy in the Caucasian area was the Tolstoy of the time, the ancestor of the writer who was himself later to serve in and write of such campaigns. In 1722 Peter transported an army by sea from Astrakhan to the Daghestan coast, and occupied territory up to Baku. But the Russians were gradually forced over the period 1729 to 1735 to abandon all the provinces they had annexed, including Derbent and Baku – which were not to return to Russian domination till the nineteenth century. Thus in 1735 the Russians were in much the same position as they had been in the 1570s. They had a few forts and a few Cossack establishments on the Terek, and the Kabarda mountaineers, theoretically in submission to the Tsar, were in fact practically independent.

But in 1777 Catherine II approved a project for establishing the 'line of the Caucasus' – a series of military forts and Cossack settlements extending up the valley of the Terek to the Sea of Azov. In 1779 the lords of Great and Little Kabarda made their submission.

Georgia had collapsed into anarchy in the eighteenth century, when King Irakli succeeded in forming a fair-sized state in Central Georgia, round Tbilisi. And in 1783 he secured a treaty by which Russia guaranteed Georgia's territorial integrity, while Georgia accepted certain limitations on her conduct of foreign affairs. Irakli died in 1798. In 1801 Paul I annexed Georgia.

The races which had sought Russian support against the Turks and Persians were the Christian Georgians (the Mohammedan Georgians remaining strongly anti-Russian) and the Christian (and Indo-European) Ossetians. And the Kabardines were already inclined to the Russian alliance. The Russian expansion therefore followed two routes. Physical geography made advance along the Caspian coast simple once the key point of Derbent had been taken – particularly as the Russians always had command of the sea on the Caspian, which they did not on the Black Sea until a later date. The other route depended on political geography as much as physical, lying through the territory of the Ossetians to the frontier of the Georgians, across what is now the Caucasian military highway, from Vladikavkaz to Tbilisi, the key points for them here being secured by their allies. By 1828 almost the whole of the present Transcaucasia was Russian, leaving in the rear of it two large independent territories. On the eastern flank lay the Chechens, Ingushi and mountain Daghestani, and on the western the great stretch of Circassian Abkhazia.

In 1828–9 the Russians fought the first major Caucasian campaign against the Turks. Poti and Anapa were captured – the Russians at this time had command of the Black Sea owing to Navarino, an advantage they did not enjoy in the subsequent Caucasian wars. They were also victorious on the main front, where the major resistance came from Mohammedan Georgians; and they gained a certain amount of territory at the peace, in particular annexing the region inhabited by these people – Meskhetia, in the mountains south of Georgia proper.

The two great Mohammedan centres behind the Russian lines were very different in character. The Circassians were ruled by great Beys and landowners and were in constant contact with Turkey. The Chechens and Ingushi, who lived a more democratic life in their wild mountainous territory, had become

Russia's Southward Expansion
1762 – 1864

attached to the puritan and egalitarian Muridist movement, which somewhat resembled the contemporary Wahabi. The Chechens had already come out on religious grounds against the Russians in the Russo-Turkish war of 1769. In 1830, the Murid, Imam Kazi Mullah, raised the country, already irritated by punitive expeditions. Several Russian detachments were destroyed, the Caucasian Line was pierced at several points, and towns beyond the Terek were raided. The campaign following lasted three years before the Russians captured Gimri, the Murid capital, and killed the Imam.

The next Imam was the famous Shamil, who revived the guerrilla war. In 1837 the Russians made a serious attempt to destroy both Circassian and Murid resistance. Russian forces suffered heavy losses on both fronts. By 1840, the Circassians, after storming a number of Russian strongholds, had been defeated and were in a difficult position, when the Murid danger made the Russians suspend operations in Circassia to concentrate all their forces against Shamil. He had inflicted heavy losses in various minor actions between 1840 and 1842. In 1843 the Muridists gained even bigger successes, including the capture of some forty guns, and attracted thousands of new recruits. The Russians were compelled to evacuate the whole of Chechniya and many points in Daghestan. They now concentrated 30,000 men and a large artillery force, the largest army that could be maintained in the area, against Shamil, and in 1845 the major attack was launched. It was an unmitigated disaster for the Russians, who lost 4,000 men and most of their baggage train in the famous Dargo campaign.

When the Crimean War started in 1853 Shamil and the Circassians were both unsubdued. Shamil immediately raided Georgia and the Russians were compelled to divert large forces from the Turkish front. In 1854 the Turks landed troops in Abkhazia and the tribes there rose against the Russians. In the same year Shamil made a more serious attack on Georgia but was defeated. In 1856, when the war ended, the Russians were able to concentrate their armies against the Chechens and Daghestanis just as after the previous war.

The fight against Shamil had now gone on for a quarter of a century and the Chechens were at the end of their resources. A Russian writer of the 1850s says, 'In the subjugation of Chechniya, the population of Lesser Chechniya – the plains – was halved between 1847 and 1850, and by 1860 had been reduced to a quarter.'[1] Shamil now surrendered.

In Circassia there had been continual trouble between the local population and the Russian settlers who had appropriated their land. By 1860, when the whole of the rest of the Caucasus had been subdued, there were still Circassians living in complete independence as far north as the Kuban River. A first attempt to make the Circassians emigrate to Turkey or to other regions of the Russian Empire was only partly successful and a new national Circassian government was set up in Sochi. But the Russian forces could now be concentrated against the Circassians and in 1862 the attack began. The fighting continued for two years, and finally some 600,000 Circassians were expelled from their country and it was settled with Russian subjects.

Thus was carried out Nicholas I's order for 'the pacification once and for all of the mountain peoples, or the shooting of the disobedient'. The story of the émigré Circassians shows the remarkable unity of the Muslim world. They played an important part in many countries in the Middle East. The Mamelukes, for instance, were Circassians not only in their origins but also in their recruitment. Their women were also celebrated throughout the harems of the area. And by this combination of sex and soldiering the race achieved great prominence. They are now scattered throughout the old Turkish Empire.

The reduction of the North Caucasus thus came half a century after Georgia to the south of it had accepted Russian rule. This resistance was, in fact, as bitter and determined as has ever been made – even leaving aside the military genius of Shamil. But the subdued peoples did not regard the matter as final. When Russia and Turkey again went to war in 1877 further revolts took place and in all six and a half Russian divisions had to be detached to the North Caucasus. The Turks again landed troops in Abkhazia and were supported by a major rising. In Chechniya a new Imam was proclaimed. The rising was temporarily suppressed, largely owing to the superiority o the new Russian rifle, but it flared up again and was only put down after considerable fighting.

In 1905 there was trouble in Chechniya, and in 1917 the collapse of the Tsarist regime led to the proclamation of a new Imam, Najmudin Gotsinski, and a more powerful figure, the Emir of Chechniya, Sheikh Uzun Hadji, who followed the Shamil tradition of theocratic democracy. It was only in 1920 that the mountaineers' resistance was crushed.

Such is a general account of how the Russians came into contact with the nations to the south of them, and finally conquered them. It is a story of a powerful military empire suppressing, with considerable difficulty, the desperate and ever-renewed resistance of peoples reluctant to give up their independence. The 1917 October revolution, it was often proclaimed, removed all these grievances of the non-Russian peoples and satisfied their national aspirations.

2

IN THE MOUNTAINS

FOUR of the nations we are dealing with inhabited the northern slopes of the Caucasus. They were the Chechens, the Ingushi, the Karachai and the Balkars. In numbers they comprised a third of the total deportees. The Chechens were the largest single people to suffer deportation. With the closely related Ingushi, who formed part of the same Chechen-Ingush Autonomous Soviet Socialist Republic, they totalled just half a million in 1939 (Chechens 407,690, Ingushi 92,074). Partly for this reason I have often taken them as representative, when it is wished to illustrate some point which applies equally to all the deportees. Thus, in this chapter, certain themes are developed at some length which, to avoid repetition, are more briefly put in the case of nations sent into exile from other areas.

Lermontov begins *Princess Mary* – the main section of his *Hero of Our Own Times* – with a description of the Caucasian landscape as seen from Pyatigorsk, where the view southwards includes the stretch from Mount Elbrus, in the Karachai-Balkar country, to Mount Kazbek on the borders of Ingushetia:

11 May   Yesterday I reached Pyatigorsk, and found rooms just inside the town on high ground at the foot of Mashuk. If rough weather comes, the clouds will lap my roof. When I opened the window at five o'clock this morning, the room was filled with the scent of flowers that were growing in the little front garden. Branches of cherry blossom peer in at the window, and the wind sometimes scatters the white petals over my writing-table. The view in three directions is splendid. Westward are the five blue peaks of Beshtu, looking (to quote Pushkin) like the vestiges of a scattered thunderstorm.

To the north the horizon is blocked by Mashuk, which re-resembles a Persian fur-cap. The eastern prospect is comparatively gentle, for below me here lies the clean, new-built town, from which rise the murmur of the medicinal springs and the voices of the cosmopolitan crowd. Beyond, the hills, blue and hazy in the distance, form an amphitheatre, fringed by the silvery chain of the snows that stretch from Mount Kazbek to the twin summits of Elbrus.

It is delightful to live in such a place. An agreeable feeling pervades my whole body. The air is pure and fresh as a child's kiss. The sun shines brightly, and there is not a cloud to dim the sky . . . .

Such, in one of the many fine descriptions of it in Russian literature, is the area where the Chechens, the Ingushi, the Karachai and the Balkars lived among the group of little nations whose homelands lie in the northern sweep of the great mountain chain.

At first sight the ethnology of the northern Caucasus is an almost incomprehensible puzzle. But we can deal with it quite simply. In the first place we can ignore for the purposes of this book the most complex area – multinational Daghestan. That leaves us, strung along between the Daghestan frontier on the south-east and the Adygei Autonomous Province to the north-west, four linguistic groups:

(a) Turkic – the Karachai and Balkars
(b) Iranian – the Ossetians
(c) the Chechens and Ingushi
(d) the Adygei (Circassian) of which different dialects form the speech of the Adygei Autonomous Province, of the former Cherkess Autonomous Province, and of the Kabardines.

(c) and (d) are distantly connected, and are purely Caucasian, having no representatives outside the area.

It will be seen that the deportees, from this part, consisted of groups (a) and (c). The Christianized and Indo-European speaking Ossetians have always been pro-Russian; while the

Circassian groups are historically the pro-Russian rump of a larger nation now mainly dispersed.

Although national characteristics in the North Caucasus seem so divisive, there has always been a degree of unity among at least the Mohammedan races there. We find in the Caucasian stories of Lermontov and Tolstoy the non-Turkic nations speaking 'Tatar' as a lingua franca – as for instance the Kabardines in Lermontov's *Bela*. (The dialect in general use was Kumyk, a Turkic language of Daghestan.) Tolstoy's stories of the Caucasian campaign, in which he himself served, show, time and again, the unity in action among the mountain peoples achieved by the Murids: three or four nationalities, again speaking 'Tatar' among themselves, are found together in raiding parties. G. J. Georgi, writing in the 1790s, describes the Caucasian tribes separately, but also puts them all together under the heading 'Mountain Tatar'. Later writers use this term to cover the Karachai, the Balkars, the Ingushi, the Chechens, and the Abazins and Kumyks of Daghestan.

The conquest of the Caucasus has always been for Russian nationalism most significant and symbolic in the imagination, far more so than the annexations of Central Asia and in the Far East. Raising the symbols of Russian imperial power on the great mountains has been highly regarded as a demonstration of might, and exalted as such by those Russians who admire such a thing. Of course, a large country's manifest destiny to rule other areas may thrill its own nationals, but it is less likely to appeal to the local inhabitants. The idea of the 'Russian Caucasus' appears in the poets and novelists who came to the area – in Pushkin, Lermontov and even Tolstoy. As Walter Kolarz says, in Lermontov particularly the idea of the Caucasus is interpreted as 'a whole period of Russian history and a political programme strongly flavoured with romanticism'. Lermontov did indeed regret the passing of the free life of the mountaineers but he prophesied (wrongly as it turned out) that the Circassians would be proud to say, 'We may truly be slaves, but at least we are slaves of the ruler of the universe!' Pushkin too treated the subjection of the mountaineers as a historical necessity. In his *Caucasian Prisoner*, even though

The Pre-deportation Ethnography of the North Caucasus

speaking of the Russian General Kotlyarevski as 'the scourge of the Caucasus. . . . Your way, like a black plague, lost and annihilated tribes', he exalts the conquest and calls on the Caucasus to 'tremble, for Yermolov comes'.

This is not the place for a complete description of the customs and ways of life of the North Caucasian nations, and it will be sufficient if the reader envisages mountaineers, intensely loyal to Mohammedanism in its most egalitarian forms, quick to resent injury, intelligent, and devoted to their independence. In the valleys a skilled and specialized agriculture was practised, with special repute for orchards and bee-keeping. Many of the *auls* or villages were fortified strong-points on the spurs of the mountains. Beyond lay the great forests into which the warrior groups could retreat from the Russian artillery. Flocks pastured on the higher slopes, to which, for instance, the shepherd nation of Balkars was virtually confined.

When Yermolov established his greatest fortress, Grozny – 'the Terrible' – it was in the Chechen territory and was designed to overawe that largest and most martial of the mountain nations. The Chechens and Ingushi have evidently been in the Caucasus for several millennia, resisting the efforts of a series of long-lived but nevertheless mortal empires to destroy them. It was left to Stalin to attempt finally to eradicate this ancient race from its ancient home.

National tradition has the Chechens descend from the legendary hero Turpalo-Nokhchou. A song about him, surviving in our own times, is quoted in the book *On the Basic Problems of Chechniya* (Grozny, 1930):

> Like sparks struck from steel
> We sprang from Turpalo-Nokhchou.
> We were born in the night
> When the she-wolf bore her litter.
> We will not lose the glory
> Of the name of our father
> Turpalo-Nokhchou.

The ideal of the Chechens – and by and large of all the mountaineers – was the *dzhigit* – equivalent of the Homeric 'hero' or the Amerindian 'brave', but always associated too with the idea of fine horsemanship.

There are many descriptions of the Chechens, some by English travellers, in the earlier part of the nineteenth century. They mainly dwell on their qualities as raiders and fighters. A more essential point is brought out by the French anthropologist, Ernest Chantre, writing in 1887:

> In the days of their independence the Chechens were grouped in separate communities administered by a National Assembly. Today they constitute a single people having no consciousness of class distinctions. In this they are very different from the Circassians, among whom the nobility has a dominating position.... Among the inhabitants of the eastern Caucasus there is complete equality. The powers with which they invest their elected Elders in Council are limited both in time and in extent.... The Chechens are gay and intelligent. The Russian officers call them the French of the Caucasus.*

It was this egalitarianism that went with the desperate resistance to Tsarist conquest, recognized by the Russian soldiery themselves – as in *A Hero of Our Own Times* where Lermontov has a veteran describing the Chechens as people, 'who, though robbers and rogues, are at any rate desperate blades'. The soldier goes on to say:

> Well, old man, they were cut-throats there, if you like! Now, thanks be, the times are peaceful; but I've seen the days when, if you went a hundred paces outside the walls you'd come across a shaggy devil on watch, and you had to keep your eyes skinned if you didn't want to get a lasso round your neck or a bullet in the back of your head. Fine fellows, they were!

Lermontov has another veteran say:

> I've seen some of them at work, cut all to pieces, riddled like a sieve with bayonet wounds, but they go on using their swords as if there were nothing the matter.

* *Recherches Anthropologiques dans le Caucase* (Lyon, 1885-7).

The smaller Ingushi nation, recognized as no less liberty-loving than their neighbours from the time when their semi-legendary forebear Kertskhal founded Nazran, right up to their Borovoye revolt in the deportation area in 1945, was also thought of as a virtuous people. In his *Ingushi* (Moscow, 1925), for instance, Prof. N. Yakovlev quotes an unnamed researcher of the previous century to the effect that 'the Ingushi are less inclined than the others to robbery; they are respected as good and honest people'.

The Ingushi lived in the western strip of the republic, with Nazran as their main town. Their mountain *auls* are specially known for the defensive towers or turrets which dominate them. But their territory is on the whole less defensible than that of Chechniya proper, and they have been subjected to the Georgians, in the eleventh century, and the Kabardines in the fifteenth, apart from the later conqueror. They always offered strenuous resistance.

Lermontov describes the *dzhigits* as they appeared to the outside observer. Tolstoy goes to the heart of the matter when he recounts the motives of Chechen-Ingush irreconcilability. In his *Hadji Murad* he describes a Russian army raid on a village of the Chechens. Houses, trees and hay are burnt, children killed, and the fountain and the mosque polluted. When the Chechens return from the mountains where they have taken refuge:

No one spoke of hatred of the Russians. The feeling experienced by all the Chechens, from the youngest to the oldest, was stronger than hate. It was not hatred, for they did not regard those Russian dogs as human beings, but it was such repulsion, disgust, and perplexity at the senseless cruelty of these creatures, that the desire to exterminate them – like the desire to exterminate rats, poisonous spiders, or wolves – was as natural an instinct as that of self-preservation.

The inhabitants of the *aul* were confronted by the choice of remaining there and restoring with frightful effort what had been produced with such labour and had been so lightly and senselessly destroyed, facing every moment the possibility of a repetition of what had happened; or to submit to the Russians – contrary to their religion and despite the repulsion and contempt they felt for them. The old men prayed, and unanimously decided to send envoys to Shamil asking him for help.

This may stand for the whole resistance of the nations of the conquered periphery of Russia, unquenched to this day.

In the early days of the Soviet regime a good view was taken of the Chechens, and their history was presented in a favourable light. The first edition of the *Large Soviet Encyclopaedia* has long articles on the Chechens and Chechniya and may be quoted as typical of the then Soviet view of the Tsarist conquest. It is interesting in several respects – in comparison with what was said later about the progressive nature of Tsarist annexation, in condemning strongly actions later carried out by the Communists in their turn, and in giving certain details which, to avoid repetition, have not been brought into the brief historical summary in Chapter 1.

After mentioning that among the Chechens 'Feudal relations ... were not developed', the articles goes on:

An extraordinary stubborn struggle with the settlers of Tsarism was carried on by the mountaineers from the end of the eighteenth century (1785–1859). The most active and powerful opponents of the Tsarist government of the conquest of northern Caucasia may justly be considered to be the Chechens. The pressure of Tsarist forces on the mountaineers brought about their unity in the struggle for their independence. And in this struggle of the mountaineers the Chechens played the most distinguished role, providing the main fighting forces and supplies for the Gazava (Holy Wars). Chechniya was the 'granary' of the Gazava.

The article goes on to describe the rise of the Mansur Ushurma, the first Imam, who fought the Russians for six years (1785–91), and his successor Kazi Mullah. It then deals with the greatest of Caucasian heroes, Shamil:

But the struggle reached its greatest force in the epoch of

the remarkable leader of the mountaineers, Shamil (1834–1859) who, basing himself on a broad national movement, was able brilliantly to organize the active resistance to Tsarism, not only by force of his military talents, but also by force of the social and political reforms carried out by him.

In the course of the war

The generals of Nicholas, after a series of defeats, realized that the way to defeat the mountaineers lay through Chechniya. There began a methodic squeezing out of the Chechens by roads through the valleys, the destruction of villages, the chopping down of woods, the construction of fortresses and the resettlement of the 'liberated lands' by Cossack stanitsas. The people, ruined by war, deprived of half their best lands, were still not defeated (1859). As a culmination the most vital elements of the population were deported to Turkey to the number of over 20,000, and were in fact destined in their majority to dying out (1865). But Chechniya seethed: in 1867 there broke out the powerful rising of the Kuata-Hadjintsi. Chechniya rose again in 1877 in connection with the Russo-Turkish war. The risings drew on themselves cruel executions and masses of victims, the annihilation of auls and the destruction of crops.

The article goes on to speak of later years and

the systematic expropriation of the mountain lands continued after the subjugation of the mountaineers. The lands of the Chechens were distributed to Cossacks, military and civil officials who had taken part in the subjugation of Chechniya, and others.

In addition 'in order to weaken the subjugated people, the government carried out the transfer of the most restive of the population', and in particular those from 'inaccessible mountain areas', to places where the Russian government would more easily be able to 'set up supervision of them'. The article tells how they became economically exploited, with the result that in the 1905 revolution they made 'armed attempts' to reclaim their lands. The result was 'more executions and the deportation of hundreds of families to Siberia'.

The general theme of this article (which it has been thought worth quoting at some length as typical of what was said in pre-war Soviet publications about minority history) is the same as that of various shocked references to Tsarist oppression made by high Soviet authority, and especially by Stalin himself. In his classic on nationality matters he says:

> The old government, the landlords and the capitalists have left us as a heritage such browbeaten peoples as . . . the Chechens. . . . These peoples were doomed to incredible suffering and to extinction.[1]

And again, in the *Thesis on the National Question* presented by Lenin to the Tenth Congress of the Russian Communist Party, it is stated that

> These 10,000,000 individuals, Kirgiz, Bashkirs, Chechens, Ossetians, Ingushi, were right up till recently methodically dispossessed of their best lands by Russian colonists. Driven gradually into sterile deserts these people were devoted to certain death.

The next twenty-five years were to prove an ironic commentary on this theme.

AFTER THE REVOLUTION

At the time of the Revolution many promises were made to the minority peoples, and often by name to those later deported. Only the week after the seizure of power the Soviet government issued a *Declaration of Rights of the Peoples of Russia* (still declared to be the basis of Communist national policy) which went to the length of admitting the right of subject races to express their wishes by rebellion:

> If any nation whatsoever is retained as part of a given State by force, if, despite its expressed desire – whether expressed in the press, in popular assemblies, in the decisions of political parties, *or by rebellions and insurrections against national oppression*

[my italics] – it has not the right of choosing freely – the troops of the annexing or, generally, the more powerful nation being completely withdrawn and without any pressure being brought to bear – the constitutional forms of its national existence, then its incorporation is an annexation, that is, seizure and coercion.[2]

Soon afterwards the government issued an appeal, signed by Lenin:

Moslems of Russia, Tatars of the Volga and the Crimea, Kirgiz and Sarts of Siberia and Turkestan, Turks and Tatars of Transcaucasia, Chechens and mountain Cossacks! All you, whose mosques and shrines have been destroyed, whose faith and customs have been violated by the Tsars and oppressors of Russia! Henceforward your beliefs and customs, your national and cultural institutions are declared free and inviolable! Build your national life freely and without hindrance. It is your right. Know that your rights, like those of all the peoples of Russia, will be protected by the might of the Revolution, by the councils of Workers', Soldiers', and Peasants' Deputies![3]

The article on the Chechen Autonomous Province in the first edition of the *Large Soviet Encyclopaedia*, already referred to, gives a partisan account of Chechniya in the Revolution, which yet presents much of the reality of the struggle which now took place in the mountains.

At first 'labouring Chechniya did not stand finally on the road of Soviet power' on account of a period of 'bourgeois nationalist movements, under the leadership of "their own" sheikhs, kulaks and capitalists'. These set up 'at the beginning of the February revolution, in Grozny, a Chechen Congress, which elected a national committee of sheikhs, officers and merchants'. In May a 'Mountain Congress' in Vladikavkaz was also taken part in by the 'reactionary nationalist elements of Chechniya'. This set up a 'Central Committee of the Union of Mountaineers' of a bourgeois-feudal character. Moreover the 'chauvinist counter-revolutionary leaders turned the Chechens against Russians in general', influencing 'the peasant masses and sometimes even the workers (through Mensheviks and S.R.'s taking part in the Grozny Soviet) among the Chechens'. The Chechens armed themselves in every way. Units recalled from the Wild Division brought their weapons.

Detachments of 'self-defenders' falling under the control of kulaks and sheikhs (Ali Mitaev and others) disarmed soldiers returning from the Caucasian Front, and seized weapons left in fortresses by soldiers of the garrisons who had returned from there to the motherland (Vedeno, Vozdvizhenka). In this period there took place mass attacks by Chechens against the Cossack stanitsas and at the same time attacks by the Cossacks on the Chechen auls. . . . In the middle of November 1917, a formal battle took place between units of the Chechen regiment and Russians, mainly Cossack units, which finished in a mass pogrom of the Chechens in Grozny, who in their turn raised the cry of nationalism in Chechniya. At the head of the national committee stood the reactionary sheikh Deni Arsanov. The town was surrounded. In their turn the inhabitants of Grozny dug themselves in. . . . Sheikh Arsanov himself, while attempting negotiations about peace with the Cossack leaders, was surprised and annihilated by them with all his band of Murids, fifty in all, in Grozny station. A second episode from these days: when units of the 111th Regiment, in charge of the Vozdvizhenka fortress, were demobilized, leaving it and returning to their country, the Chechens from neighbouring auls took the fortress, destroyed the barracks and churches and other stone buildings, expelled the Russian inhabitants to Grozny and themselves settled the place.

The *Encyclopaedia* continues:

At the end of 1917 the leaders of the Cossacks of the Mozdok Province in congress, attempted to create a bloc of all Russians against the Chechens and Ingushis, declaring themselves to be on the side of the Soviet power. This provocational tactic was unmasked only by the small, but influential, Bolshevik delegation to the congress (Kirov and others). The

B

Central Committee of the Union of United Mountaineers openly joined the counter-revolutionaries, the so-called South-eastern Union of Cossack Armies, Mountaineers of the Caucasus and Free Peoples of the Steppe.

In January 1918, the article goes on, 'a so-called "Atagoi Soviet" was organized in Chechniya, in which the predominating influence was obtained by the priesthood and kulaks standing on the positions of zoological nationalism'. However, this body was finally, by a series of developments and splits, turned into an organization supporting the Soviet regime. What in fact seems to have happened is fairly simple; when the Chechens thought that the Cossacks and Russians were pro-Soviet they themselves became anti-Soviet. As soon as the counter-revolutionary movement started winning over the local Russians and Cossacks the Chechens turned to the other side.

'A most important role among the pioneers of the Soviet movement in Chechniya was played by Sergo Ordzhonikidze . . .' and by February 1918, the article continues, 'a leading local Communist, A. Sheripov, declared that the overwhelming majority of the Chechen people was ready to fight for the Soviet power.' Sheripov headed 'Chechen units of the Red Army' which 'took part in the battles of the Grozny workers against the Cossack counter-revolutionaries'. Severe fighting took place, and 'in February 1919 the Soviet forces left Grozny'. The White armies were by this time fully organized and in control of most of South Russia. The Chechens continued to fight them in the mountains. 'Hundreds and thousands of poor Chechens devotedly fought against the White Guard regiments and artillery, suffering heavy losses.' The *Encyclopaedia* claims Bolshevik leadership for some of this resistance, but admits that 'a new movement of labouring Chechniya was called up. But at first the masses were under the flag of the Shariya.'

The Shariya, the Islamic system of law and custom which had been implicitly guaranteed by the Appeal of December 1917, is here treated as a hostile influence. But at the time Stalin stated directly, with specific reference to the Chechens and Ingushi and the other mountain peoples:

If it is shown that the Shariya is necessary, then let the Shariya remain. The Soviet Government has no thought of declaring war on the Shariya.[4]

To return to the *Encyclopaedia*, it describes the movement based on Islamic and national feeling which now arose:

The movement was headed by the fanatical sheikh, well known in the mountains, Uzun Hadji, Imam and Emir of the North Caucasian Emirate .... Uzun Hadji opened active war against the army of Denikin, and a 'united front' of its own sort was proposed to him by the leaders of Soviet Chechniya, Sheripov and Gikalo, in this struggle against Denikin, with the preservation of wholly independent Red units. At the same time they did not give up their work of unmasking the social face of Uzun Hadji. The movement was so important that the Denikinists were compelled to detach large forces to the Chechen front.

The *Encyclopaedia* goes on to describe a struggle for influence between the Bolsheviks and Uzun Hadji with the result that, not unnaturally, the 'Uzun Hadjist movement showed its true face . . . carrying out policies openly hostile to the Bolsheviks'. The 'bourgeois nationalists' were still, however, fighting in collaboration with Red units in September 1919, and it was only on 31 January 1920 that the leaders 'showed their counter-revolutionary face' and then only by failing to assist a small Communist force attacked by a larger White unit. Open fighting broke out shortly afterwards and at first the Communists had to retreat into Georgia. But 'in March 1920, in Chechniya, Soviet power was finally celebrated'.

Though this account, to put it mildly, requires supplementing from other sources, it gives a fair impression of the main moves in the struggle for power in the mountains, and indicates pretty plainly the essence of the matter: that the Chechens and Ingushi were the mainstay of the struggle against the Whites, that they were at first prepared to take the Bolsheviks at their face value, that they then became disillusioned and went into open opposition, and that they were subdued from outside.

That the Ingushi, in particular, had supported the Bolsheviks wholeheartedly at the critical moment was gratefully admitted by Ordzhonikidze, the Bolshevik leader in the area, in a speech in December 1918:

> I recall the moment . . . when our fate hung on a hair; this was a moment . . . when we had no following . . . when we were looked upon with timidity . . . when only the Ingushi followed us without hesitation.[5]

The post-revolution organization of the North Caucasus split the area in two. The mountain tribes of Daghestan were united with the Russified plain stretching up to and north of the Terek River. The Chechens and Ingushi, whose closest ties were with the Avars in mountain Daghestan, were detached from them and united with the other nations to the north-westward. This second republic – 'The Mountain Republic' – united the Chechens, Ingushi, Ossetians, Kabardines, Balkars and Karachai. Each of these six nations formed a district, Stalin having said:

> Each of these peoples – Chechens, Ingushi, Ossetians, Kabardines, Balkars, Karachai, and also the Cossacks who remain within the autonomous mountain territory – should have its National Soviet to administer the affairs of the given people in accordance with its manner of life.[6]

The towns of Grozny and Vladikavkaz were given separate status.*

---

* The history of the Mountain ASSR may be briefly stated in terms of the elements into which it was broken up. In September 1921 Kabarda was removed from it and turned into an autonomous province. In January 1922 the Karachai were taken from it and given a joint autonomous province with the Cherkess, with a capital at Batalpashinsk: at the same time the Balkars were merged into a Kabardine-Balkar autonomous province with Nalchik for capital. In December 1922 the Chechens were given an autonomous province of their own. This left only the Ossetians and the Ingushi who were separated in July 1924, thus completing the disintegration of the Republic. Further changes were the breaking up of the Karachai-Cherkess autonomous province into two in April 1926 and the re-unification of the Chechens and Ingushi into a single province in January 1934. In December 1936 the Kabardine-Balkar, Chechen-Ingush and North Ossetian provinces became Autonomous Republics.

In April 1921, a congress took place at Vladikavkaz after which a telegram was sent to Stalin, Commissar for Nationalities, saying that 'liberated from the yoke of the oppressor the mountaineers of the Caucasus, Chechens, Ingushi, Ossetians, Dighors*, Balkars and Karachai on this memorable day are all animated with the ardent desire finally to conquer world imperialism which holds in slavery millions of orientals'. The executive committee of thirteen members set up seems to have contained nine Russians, two from the always pro-Russian Ossetians, one Ingush and one of doubtful nationality.

The mountain peoples had had a considerable amount of troubles among themselves at various times in their history. Nevertheless, when left alone they had shown a surprising capacity for unity. Shamil had been welcomed throughout the area, except by the Christian Ossetians. In 1917–20 all these nations had found it possible to co-operate in a single political unit. And the Soviet Government had originally recognized the advantages in setting up the Mountain Republic. That form of organization had, indeed, a progressive air to it. And the federation of the small peoples might have been expected to give a broader local loyalty than the division later enforced.

The Soviet authorities, on the other hand, soon abandoned federal solutions in complicated national areas. The main case of this was the dissolution in 1936 of the Transcaucasian Soviet Federal Socialist Republic, which had united Georgia, Armenia and Azerbaidzhan. The erection one by one of all the Turkic nations of Turkestan into separate Union Republics had something of the same effect. What happened in all these cases was that local unity was halted and the administration of each area was linked direct to Moscow, so that there could be no question of any joint opposition on party or governmental level against the proposals of the Soviet Government, and no development of local solidarity in any way. Moreover local cultural unities were broken up where they existed. The idea of a unified Turkic language in Central Asia was greatly discouraged and each local dialect was differentiated as far as possible from that of its neighbours, while at the same time being Russianized. In the

*A branch of the Ossetians.

North Caucasus there was no linguistic unity, but such elements of it as existed were discouraged. The languages generally understood in the North Caucasus were Turkic (Kumyk Tatar) on the one hand, and (in connection with the religious schools) Arabic, to a lesser extent, on the other. Soviet education has concentrated on substituting Russian as the tongue in which the Circassian speaks to the Chechen, just as it is through Moscow that he must make his political approach to members of the neighbouring nations.

In the years between the revolution and the deportation, Soviet sources are less inclined to refer to the scale of the troubles which continually flared up in the mountains. The resistance of 'kulak and mullah elements' to collectivization and to Soviet national policy is mentioned occasionally. And more may be guessed from such references as this to the resistance to comparatively mild changes like the (temporary) introduction of the Latin alphabet in the late twenties:

> The same resistance to latinization emanated also from the home-bred sheikhs, murids and mullahs in Daghestan and among the mountain peoples of North Caucasia. The latter, led by Sheikh Ali Mitaev, drawing on the services of their hirelings (bandit elements), met literally with daggers drawn the first copies of the Soviet alphabets in the new script which appeared in the mountain villages. The hunger strike proclaimed by the Chechen mullahs in protest against latinization was a characteristic token of this opposition.
>
> We observe, too, the same scene of counter-action on the part of Ibrahim Valiev's supporters in the Crimea, who in every way sabotaged and tried to discredit the idea of latinization.[7]

There were many complaints of the influence of Islam – that, for instance, the Ingushi, including many members of the Communist Party, were completely under Islamic influence, even the children refusing to touch atheist textbooks (*Anti-religioznik*, No. 11, 1931).

That these changes were enforced by Russian officials is also clear from complaints like the following, which were occasionally allowed to appear in those days:

> In the apparatus of the Chechen-Ingush Provincial Executive Committee are officials who know neither the Chechen nor the Ingush language.[8]

A decree of 7 January 1936 reveals that of 1,310 officials in the North Caucasus territory, only 17 were of the mountain nationalities. This led to misunderstandings, which are given as part of the reason why the local soviets in Chechniya failed to carry out government orders.[9] Troubles had become so acute that Kalinin in person paid a visit and urged reconciliation.[10]

The idea of the North Caucasus which remained in the minds of the Stalinists may be seen from statements made at the trial of Bukharin and others in 1938. Evidence was given by V. I. Ivanov, who had been Second Secretary in the North Caucasus in 1928–31, that he had acted there as an agent of the Rightist opposition. Bukharin, he said, had told him that 'the northern Caucasus would play a very important part in our struggle against the Party and the Soviet power' and again 'we must make it our task to transform the northern Caucasus into a Russian Vendée'. The formation of insurrectionary bands is also mentioned.[11] In his evidence Rykov, former Prime Minister of the Soviet Union, also mentioned the plotters' 'special attention to the North Caucasus' because *inter alia* of 'the specific character of its traditions and also in view of its political and economic importance as a region bordering on the Ukraine, possessing a large number of national republics and supplying a large quantity of grain'. He refers also to 'kulak insurrections'.[12]

These remarks, which we may take as having been drafted by the regime propagandists to put into the mouths of the accused, seem to indicate official sensitivity about the North Caucasus, and also give the impression that the strong peasant resistance being shown at the time throughout the USSR was particularly powerful among the mountaineers. In drawing attention to the vulnerable nature of the area from a Soviet point of view, they seem to some extent to foreshadow the reasons for the eventual decision to deport the inhabitants.

The great majority of Soviet statements about the mountaineers, however, are ones which assert their loyalty and
happiness. For completeness, we may quote a few of these. The
Encyclopaedia article already referred to concludes:

> The Soviet power gave Chechniya autonomy, gave it
> literature, constructed tens of new schools, educated in techni-
> cal and higher educational institutions hundreds of thousands
> of young people of the mountain poor, involved thousands
> of Chechen peasants in industry, creating qualified cadres of
> the Chechen proletariat. The Chechen Autonomous Province,
> overcoming the resistance of kulak and mullah elements, who
> used in the struggle aristocratic connections and religious
> prejudices, successfully carried out the basic tasks facing the
> whole country – industrialization, the creation of kolkhozes –
> and convincingly went forward on the road of constructing a
> Socialist commonwealth.

In the last years of peace, on 15 January 1939, *Izvestia*
published the following communiqué from the Tass agency:

> Fifth anniversary of Checheno-Ingushetia. Grozny. 14
> January. Five years ago today, on 15 January 1934, two
> Caucasian peoples, the Chechens and the Ingushi, closely
> connected by their language, culture and way of life, joined
> together to form the autonomous province of the Chechen-
> Ingushi. On 5 December 1936, this province was converted
> into an Autonomous Soviet Socialist Republic. The history of
> Checheno-Ingushetia has been marred by decades of bloody
> struggle on the part of a race with a strong love of liberty
> against colonizers and the national bourgeoisie, the mainstay
> of Tsarism. But under the Soviet regime the republic has been
> so transformed as to be unrecognizable. The kolkhozes,
> within which 92·7 per cent of all agricultural undertakings
> are now combined, have been accorded a perpetual grant of
> more than 400,000 hectares of land. An important oil
> industry has been created. New oilfields have been exploited
> and two big refineries built, as well as a machine factory.
> Food factories, chemical factories and other forms of local

production have been brought into being or organized. Under the sun of the Stalin Constitution the culture of the Chechen-Ingush people, national in form but socialist in content, has made a great step forward. Before the Revolution there were only three schools in the whole of Checheno-Ingushetia. Today there are 342 primary and secondary schools accommodating 118,000 pupils. Hundreds of engineers and teachers emerge every year from the high schools, the technical schools and the workers' faculties. All these brilliant results have been achieved in the course of a bitter struggle against the enemies of the people – Trotskyites, Bukharinites and bourgeois nationalists who have sought to rob the workers of the fruits of the great October Socialist Revolution.

This formula 'national in form, socialist in content' has become a classic compression, much used in the USSR to express the essence of Soviet national policy. It has been cynically translated as 'the right to say what the Kremlin wants you to in your own language'. On political matters this is demonstrably the case. But it is also true that one of the most characteristic things in the life of the Soviet minorities is the care taken to provide them with a Soviet literature of their own. We shall find that all the deported nations had a flourishing production of poems – sometimes even 'folk poems' – praising the regime, collective farms, the Party and, in particular, Stalin personally. On this point, as on others, we may give a single Chechen poem in full, as typical of the sort of thing to be found everywhere, but hardly bearing repetition. Here it is:

CHECHEN SONG OF STALIN

Even if the sea were ink,
And the sky were made of paper
Who could tell the people's gladness,
Though inspired with highest fervour?
Who could express with faltering pen
Our love for you, Desired One?
Too small are the heavens and the oceans
To reveal the thoughts we hold.

You, our father and our brother,
Gave us happiness and opened
Wide the gates to future joy.
– Long life to you, beloved Stalin!
Such is our hope and prayer for you.
As the nacre hides its treasure,
Holy is the womb that bore thee.
Most happy is she above all women,
Whose child is our unfailing sun.
Like the stars so brightly shining,
You shine like the sun for us.
Your glory, spread among all peoples,
Is loudly hymned from land to land.
Stalin gave joy to us, his children,
Stalin – the dew in a thirsty land.
Flowers adorn the hills and meadows,
Flower of our hearts – no less than these.
You, our father and our brother,
Gave us happiness and opened
Wide the gates to future joy.
– Long life to you, beloved Stalin!
Such is our hope and prayer for you.
If the foe again should sharpen
His blade against the Soviet land
We shall not sleep. Just speak the word
And we shall rend them all like tigers.
Fresher than dewdrops, sweet as honey,
The Caucasus, its youth restored,
Comes to you, its people sing:
The name Stalin gleams like a star!
You, our father and our brother,
Gave us happiness and opened
Wide the gates to future joy.
– Long life to you, beloved Stalin!
Such is our hope and prayer for you.

(Translated from pp. 78–9,
Chechen-Ingush Folklore, Moscow, 1940.)

Unlike the Chechens and Ingushi, the Karachai and Balkars are not of the oldest indigenous stock. They arrived in the area from the Crimean sphere, as part of the Tatar wanderings of that time, about five hundred years ago. They were gradually driven by their larger neighbours into the alpine meadows and torrent valleys, close under the mountain glaciers, which they now mainly inhabit. To the south, at the watershed, the passes are at from 9,000–11,000 feet. The route from Klukhori into Georgia was nevertheless an old trade route in Byzantine times, though lately little used. They live mainly by sheep and cattle herding, and hunting.

Though of different stock the Karachai and Balkars had much the same history as their co-religionists, the Chechens and Ingushi. They too had offered stubborn resistance to the Tsars, especially in the 1820s, and they too had supported the Murids. And in general all that has been said about the Chechen-Ingush could be repeated about these small Turkic peoples.

The dialects of the Karachai and the Balkars are very similar, and on the basis of them a literary language – Karachai-Balkar – was developed in the twenties, when the authorities were upgrading the local Turkic dialects throughout the Union, with a view to helping prevent the rise, or the continuation, of a general Turkic sense of unity.

Though the Karachai and the Balkars live in geographical contiguity, they are separated by the mountains. Such separation has not prevented administrative unification in some other parts of the Soviet Union. For instance, a comparison of the ethnographical, physical and administrative maps of Ferghana Valley in Turkestan shows that, while ethnographical frontiers have to some extent been ignored, this has not been for reasons of physical geography; and that areas divided from one another by a series of physical barriers are nevertheless united to relatively inaccessible, rather than to their nearest, units. The same, indeed, may be seen in a less striking way in the Caucasus itself, where the Nakhichevan ASSR, with a Turkic population, forms part of Azerbaidzhan from which it is separated not merely by mountains, but actually by a broad strip of Armenian territory.

The Balkars were, up to the time of their deportation,

neither given a separate territory nor united with the Karachai. Instead they formed part of the Kabardine-Balkar ASSR with the non-Turkic Kabardines. The total population of the republic in 1939 was 359,000, which indicates that Kabardines (and Russians) were in the great majority.

That the administrative convenience of uniting Balkars and Kabardines was not overwhelming is shown by the fact that for a time in the 1920s Balkaria formed part of the Mountain Republic while Kabarda did not, and also by the fact that when the Balkars were deported in 1944 much of their territory was not then united to Kabarda, but transferred to Georgia – although the mountain division between Balkaria and Georgia is at least as high and as difficult to cross as that between Balkaria and the Karachai.

Volume 4 of the first edition of the *Large Soviet Encyclopaedia* (1926) has short articles on the Balkars and Balkaria in which the people are described as shepherds and the country defined as 'the valley of the upper course of the Cherek – in a broad sense, the whole of the southern mountain part of the Kabardine-Balkar Autonomous Province'. Volume 30 (published in 1937) has an article on the Kabardine-Balkar ASSR. Resistance to the Soviet regime in the area is said to have gone on till 1923 when 'banditism' was liquidated.

Volume 31 of the first edition (1937) of the *Encyclopaedia* also has articles on the Karachai. The population of the Karachai Autonomous Province is given as 104,400 (1933), 81 per cent of it Karachai. On the history of the people it describes their conquest by Russia as 'one of the links in the colonial campaign of Tsarism in the Caucasus'. The Russian generals had announced in 1828 that 'the resistance of the Karachai is broken'. 'But', the article goes on to say, 'the struggle of the Karachai was not ended', for they participated in Shamil's Muridist movement against the Russians. Finally their resistance was suppressed and they were 'robbed' of their economic wealth. 'National oppression and ridicule by the Tsarist government made the difficult position of the Karachai twice as hard.' 'Several risings' took place, including trouble in 1873 and 1905. In 1917 the Karachai, for a time, lived in virtual

independence. It is interesting to see how the article puts this.
It says that it 'changed only the form of rule; instead of Tsarist
agents – Atamans and Commissioners – the Karachai were
governed by exploiters from the camp of bourgeois-nationalist
elements'. This is a significant expression, applying as it would
to any country setting itself up as independent under non-
Communist rule.

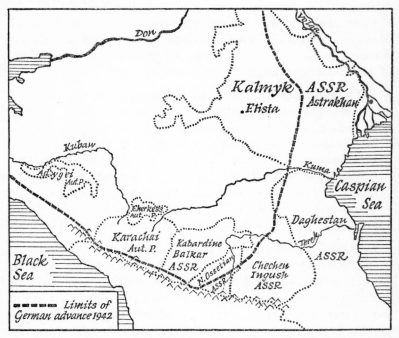

*Autonomous Republics and Provinces in the North Caucasus 1939, and
the Limits of German Advance 1942.*

The independence did not last. A detachment of the 9th
Soviet Army entered the Karachai territory in August 1920 to
'give help' to such Communists as were in the area. 'The local
counter-revolutionaries offered stubborn resistance. The
struggle lasted one and a half months.' Later trouble was put
down in 1920. The resistance of 'kulak' elements was broken
in 1930 and, later in the thirties, 1,500 members of the Karachai
Communist Party were purged as counter-revolutionary

bourgeois elements. The history of the Karachai under Soviet rule is stated in the article's peroration to be 'a clear illustration of the attainments of Leninist-Stalinist national policy' and the Karachai themselves to be 'one of the leading members of the happy family of peoples of the USSR'.

Like the Chechens, they had their Soviet literature. The article on Karachai literature in Volume 31 (1937) mentions as one of its new classics a poem of praise called 'Stalin'.

Even after the war started the same line was maintained about the mountain peoples – right up to within months of the deportations, in fact. Kalinin, Chairman of the Presidium of the USSR Supreme Soviet, declared in 1942:

> The Caucasus is the most enlightening demonstration of the reforming beneficial effect of the Soviet system on the psychology and character of people who, not without reason, saw danger to themselves everywhere. The Caucasians have now become a socialist people who see in the collective system their bulwark, the foundation of material prosperity and a higher intellectual life . . . the whole Caucasus has become one mountain village for its peoples. The whole Soviet land, from border to border, has become their beloved home.[13]

By 5 October 1942, the Chechens had won 44 decorations in the Red Army – more than several much larger nations. Even in 1943 an official Soviet history mentioned as evidence of the unity of the Soviet peoples in the war the fact that in the period from 9 December 1942 to 3 March 1943 the Chechens and the Ingushi had contributed twelve million roubles, and the Kalmyks nine million roubles for the war effort. Seven and a half million roubles had also been contributed by the Kabardines and Balkars.[14]

Thus, Soviet statements about the devotion and happiness of the Chechens and Ingushi, the Karachai and Balkars, were authoritative and repeated, throughout the peace and most of the war. After 1943 nothing seems to have been said about them, but this passed unnoticed among the eventful happenings of the end of the war, and it came as a surprise when a decree was published in *Izvestia* of 26 June 1946, reading as follows:

Law concerning the Abolition of the Chechen-Ingush Autonomous Soviet Socialist Republic and the Changing of the Crimean Autonomous Soviet Socialist Republic into the Crimean Province.

During the Great Patriotic War, when the peoples of the USSR were heroically defending the honour and independence of the Fatherland in the struggle against the German-Fascist invaders, many Chechens and Crimean Tatars, at the instigation of German agents, joined volunteer units organized by the Germans and, together with German troops, engaged in armed struggle against units of the Red Army; also at the bidding of the Germans they formed diversionary bands for the struggle against Soviet authority in the rear; meanwhile the main mass of the population of the Chechen-Ingush and Crimean ASSRs took no counter-action against these betrayers of the Fatherland.

In connection with this, the Chechens and the Crimean Tatars were resettled in other regions of the USSR, where they were given land, together with the necessary governmental assistance for their economic establishment. On the proposal of the Presidium of the Supreme Soviet of the RSFSR the Chechen-Ingush ASSR was abolished and the Crimean ASSR was changed into the Crimean Province by decrees of the Presidium of the Supreme Soviet of the USSR.

The Supreme Soviet of the Russian Soviet Federative Socialist Republic resolves:

1. To confirm the abolition of Chechen-Ingush ASSR and the changing of the Crimean ASSR into the Crimean Province.
2. To make the necessary alterations and additions to Article 14 of the Constitution of the RSFSR.

Chairman of the Presidium of the Supreme Soviet of the RSFSR,

I. Vlasov.

Secretary of the Presidium of the Supreme Soviet of the RSFSR,

P. Bakhmurov.

Moscow, The Kremlin, 25 June 1946

It was later learnt that this deportation had taken place early in 1944. No statement of any sort about the Karachai and the Balkars was ever made. Their deportation was simply deduced indirectly in the circumstances narrated in Chapter 5.

On the far side of the Georgian plains from the Caucasus proper lies the great block known as the Armenian Highlands, over which Russia and Turkey fought for more than a century. The area on the present Soviet-Turkish border from the Georgian-Armenian frontier to a point just inside the Adzhar ASSR – that is, the valleys round the upper Kura, from the Kobliani to the Tba-paravani – has, and has had, no political status of its own, but is commonly known as Meskhetia. Almost cut off from the rest of the Georgian SSR by a stretch of un-inhabited mountain, it is shown in pre-war ethnological maps as being inhabited by Kurds, Armenians, and (over the greater part of its extent) Turks, with a very few scattered Russian and Georgian settlements. The Turks concerned are referred to as 'Turks' in the 1926 Census, but as 'Azerbaidzhanis' in the 1939 one. This change seems to have been put through in 1935–6, when the local schools switched from ordinary Turkish to Azer-baidzhani. In any case, the inhabitants represent a Georgian population which became Islamised and Turkised in the seven-teenth century, and the *Large Soviet Encyclopaedia*, First Edition (in an article 'Samtskhe-Saatabago'), describes them as such. Anatolian Turkish and Azerbaidzhani, of the Oghuz group of Turkic dialects, differ only slightly, but the Meskhetians are in fact best described as Turkish (though a few thousand Karapa-pakhs, more Azerbaidzhani in speech, were also settled in the area and shared the fate of the others). The local Armenians, known as Khemshils, are also Turkised. In fact the population was one which might be thought to have Turkish sympathies, even though in border areas of overlapping ethnic populations it has normally been the Soviet claim that, on the contrary, the Sovietized section of a given people is the one which those on the other side envy and wish to join.

On 15 November 1944, this mixed population was deported. It was not alleged against them that they had collaborated with the Germans – who had not come within hundreds of miles of the area. In fact, the move was represented as not being of a penal nature at all, but as a matter of evacuating them from an area which might be reached by the enemy.[15]

But by this time there was no question of the Germans, then on the point of defeat, being the real threat. The political and strategic motive was plainly – already – with a view to trouble with Turkey and the West. And, in fact, within the year articles were appearing in the USSR claiming the Soviet right over Georgian and other minority areas in north-east Turkey.

In the Meskhetian case, it was not even possible to deduce the deportation from Soviet documents, as with the Balkars, Karachai and Kalmyks. There were no constitutional or administrative changes, and the post-war ethnological maps still showed Meskhetia as Turkic – perhaps because not even their compilers knew the facts. However that may be, the entire operation remained virtually unknown in the West for a quarter of a century.

3

STEPPE, PENINSULA
AND VOLGA

On the Steppe: The Kalmyks

A few hundred miles north of the well-watered and forest-covered highlands, where the egalitarian mountaineers fought for their natural rights, lived a very different people. The semi-desert steppe to the west of the Volga mouth has over its whole vast extent only a few areas, as in the Ergeni Hills, where cultivation is possible. In places great inland sand-dunes stretch for miles. The rainfall is only 4–8 inches a year. Dust storms are common.

There from the middle of the seventeenth century, a nation of tent-dwelling nomads, tending their sheep, cattle, horses and camels, lived under the rule of their Khan, appointed to reign over them by the living Buddha, the Dalai Lama in Lhasa himself. For the Kalmyks are Buddhists of the Zonkavist, or Lamaist, rite. They are also Mongols, not in some general sense, but literally: their language is virtually the same as that spoken in Mongolia proper. They used the old Mongol alphabet – indeed it was they who perfected it in 1646. Literary Mongolian was their written tongue until 1931.[1]

Soon after their arrival in the Volga area, as part of a migration from Chinese Turkestan, they became allies of the Russians, charged by Peter the Great with guarding the eastern frontier. This alliance gradually became vassalage. Finally, under Catherine the Great, they were deprived of their independence and in 1771 the Khanate was abolished.

Until that date their nation occupied, in addition to the area which later became the Kalmyk ASSR on the west bank of the Volga, an even larger territory on its eastern bank. In 1771 there occurred one of the most extraordinary events in any

50

national history. A conspiracy was formed for escaping Russian oppression by a migration. It was designed that the entire nation should head eastwards until it was removed from the Russian yoke. It was only by accident that that section of the Kalmyks on the European side of the Volga was prevented from joining the larger portion of the population in this extraordinary move.

All this is mainly known to English readers through De Quincey's essay 'Revolt of the Tartars'. He says:

> There is no great event in modern history, or, perhaps it may be said more broadly, none in all history from its earliest records, less generally known, or more striking to the imagination, than the flight eastwards of a principal Tartar nation across the boundless steppes of Asia in the latter half of the last century.

As De Quincey says, it is remarkable as a conspiracy, as a great military expedition like that of Xenophon and as a great religious exodus – for one of the Kalmyk objections to Russian rule was its persecution of their Buddhist faith.

> Then, again, in the gloomy vengeance of Russia and her vast artillery, which hung upon the rear and the skirts of the fugitive vassals, we are reminded of Miltonic images.

In January 1771 representatives of the clans assembled and they were told by the organizers of the conspiracy

> of the oppressions of Russia; of her pride and haughty disdain evidenced towards them by a thousand acts; of her contempt for their religion; of her determination to reduce them to absolute slavery; of the preliminary measures she had already taken by erecting forts upon many of the great rivers in their neighbourhood; of the ulterior intentions she thus announced to circumscribe their pastoral lands, until they would all be obliged to renounce their flocks, and to collect in towns like Sarepta, there to pursue the mechanical and servile trades of shoe-maker, tailor and weaver, such as the free-born Tartar had always disdained.

De Quincey describes how for eight months, starting in the depths of winter, the entire nation fled, attacked at every step by the Russians and their confederates, until they reached the frontiers of China where the Emperor Kien Long received them kindly and gave them land, and how he set a granite and brass column to mark the occasion of their arrival telling how 'by the favour of Kien Long, God's Lieutenant upon Earth, the ancient Children of the Wilderness – the Torgote Tartars – flying before the wrath of the Grecian Czar' found refuge.

An entire nation, amounting to 300,000 people with their women and children, had penetrated, with heavy loss, a distance of 3,000 miles. If a few of De Quincey's details are inaccurate, he conveys the feelings of the oppressed Kalmyks adequately. Those who stayed behind faced the troubles their fellow-nationals had fled to escape.

The Kalmyks remaining on the west bank of the Volga had been confined to the bare stretch between the valleys of the Volga and the Kuma. In this vast but sparsely settled area they continued, until recently, their semi-nomadic herdsmen's life, except for villages of fishermen on the low-lying Caspian coast.

It will not be worth repeating at much length for the Kalmyks (or for the other nations dealt with) the examples of the Soviet attitude given in the case of the Chechens. These are much the same for each of them. But we may briefly look at Volume 30 of the first edition of the *Large Soviet Encyclopaedia* (1937). On the history of people it speaks of 'intensive colonial robbery' by the Russians starting in 1668–71, mentions Kalmyk participation in the rebellion of 1707–8 and adds that by the end of the eighteenth century Kalmykia was wholly a colony of the Russian Empire.

Some light is thrown on the absence of class hatreds among the Kalmyks by a description of their behaviour in 1905: 'The Kalmyk peasantry, for the most part, showed itself the ideological prisoner of its own bourgeoisie, spiritual leaders and feudalists.' For the aims of these undisputed leaders of the Kalmyk people were national. They sought, the *Encyclopaedia* says, autonomy, national representation in the Duma, irrigation, the right of Kalmyks to their own territory, and so on.

In 1917, too, Kalmyk revolutionary enthusiasm was of the wrong sort and it had to be made up for by Russians: 'In 1917 the Astrakhan proletariat [i.e. *Russian* Bolsheviks] stood at the head of the revolution in the steppes.' At this time, in March 1917, a Kalmyk Congress set up a Central Committee with nationalist aims. After the revolution the Kalmyks carried out early in 1918 a 'counter-revolutionary rising against the Astrakhan workers'. A Kalmyk congress of Soviets could only be held in Astrakhan. Meanwhile the civil war raged on the Kalmyk steppe. On 2 July 1919, Lenin addressed a special letter to 'the toiling Kalmyk people'.

Part of Lenin's proclamation, not quoted in the *Encyclopaedia*, runs:

> Your land has been seized by conquerors who are fighting to restore the rights of capitalists and landowners. They are helped by British and French capitalists who oppress hundreds of millions of your co-religionists in Asia.

In retrospect it is interesting to compare the later situation of the Buddhist inhabitants of Burma and Ceylon and of Kalmykia respectively. Lenin also added, 'Kalmyk brothers, the entire past of your people is an uninterrupted chain of suffering.'

In 1919 a decree was also issued forbidding further Russian settlement in Kalmyk lands.[2] This, according to the *Encyclopaedia*, 'underlined the inviolability of Kalmyk territory'. It was followed by a political concession when in November 1920 a Kalmyk Autonomous Province was set up.

The *Encyclopaedia* article contains a number of other significant points. For instance it concedes that the Party organization in Kalmykia was only formed in 1918 and then had only 'a few members'. In 1921 the membership, including candidate members, was 609. Even in 1933 membership was only 3,143. In that year, however, the Autonomous Province became an Autonomous Soviet Socialist Republic. Kalmyk resistance had continued for a time. But 'banditism was finally liquidated in 1926'. And at the tenth Congress of the Kalmyk Soviets in 1931 it was proclaimed that 'stone by stone the indestructible foundation of the Kalmyk Socialist edifice is being laid'. During

World War II 20,000 Kalmyk soldiers were raised for the Red Army. Colonel Khomutnikov's Kalmyk Cavalry Division was praised for special gallantry at Rostov in 1942. And in October 1942 a letter from the Kalmyks to Stalin on 'the determination of the Kalmyk people to mobilize all their resources to help the Red Army rout the invader' was much quoted.

The Kalmyks were still mentioned favourably even after the final withdrawal of the Germans from their territory in January 1943. The following month the Kalmyk Provincial Committee of the Communist Party announced various measures such as the reopening of schools, and stated that the Kalmyks had collected seven million roubles for arms for the Red Army.[3]

This was the last that was heard of them for fourteen years.

As in the case of the other deported peoples a Kalmyk pro-Soviet literature had been synthesized, and, as elsewhere, the older literature was ordered to be purged.

The genuine Kalmyk epic, *Dzhangar*, described by De Quincey as 'seventeen English miles in length', was found to be 'imbued with religious and reactionary content' and it was ordered 'to be carefully purged'. Meanwhile the heroes of the *Dzhangar* were transferred to a new epic, *Yorel*, in which they assist Stalin to build 'the land of eternal youth, the land of abundance'. It concludes with an appeal to Stalin to 'lead us on to Communism'.[4]

The Kalmyks disappeared before the extremes of this method could be applied to their literature. An example of how it was performed in Stalin's later days, and in the time of his successors, may be seen in the treatment of the Kirgiz epic, *Manas*:

> The expurgation of the epic should be strictly scientific and principled. It should take into account all the historical circumstances in the life of the people. This demands a suitable selection of variants, songs and episodes, a selection of which the fundamental principle must be the preservation in the epic of all the best elements inherent in the past of the Kirgiz people.[5]

In 1956 a meeting of the Department of Social Sciences of the

Academy of Science of the Kirgiz SSR discussed the new 'composite version' of the *Manas* epic. It stated that this epic had now been purged of mysticism, narrow nationalism, etc. There were complaints, however, that the idealization of the feudal past still seeped through, and further action was recommended.[6] (Compare also *1984* by George Orwell, with its account of how it was necessary to 'produce garbled versions – definitive texts they were called' of poems which had become politically objectionable but which it was not wished to suppress entirely.)

The Kalmyks have often been treated, in spite of the distances and differences, as one of the nations of the northern Caucasus. And, indeed, nothing separates their territory and Chechniya except the even more barren steppe between the Kuma and the Terek, inhabited yet more lightly by a few Nogai Tatars. Yet there are many differences: national, in that Kalmyks are Mongols; religious, in that they are Buddhist; historical, in their much earlier subjugation; geophysical and economic, in their steppe country and its livestock economy. And, again unlike the Chechens, during the war much of their territory, including the capital Elista, was occupied by the Germans, and a number of Kalmyks followed them in their retreat.

The deportation of the Kalmyks was the only one involving an entire republic of which no public statement was ever made. It was only indirectly that it was possible to deduce that they had followed their kinsfolk of the eighteenth century eastwards, without, however, finding a friendly reception at the end of the journey. The 'integrity of the Kalmyk territory' promised by Lenin, the 'indestructible edifice' which their republic had been asserted to be, did not stand the first strains put upon them.

IN THE PENINSULA: THE CRIMEAN TATARS

Unlike the little Caucasian peoples, content merely to defend the independence of their valleys and entering Russian history simply as the victims of distant campaigns of conquest and colonization, the Tatars of the Crimea had once, as we have seen, formed a powerful and aggressive empire, often threatening Moscow itself.

They are also the most famous of the Turkic races involved. The Turkic languages are extremely close to one another. They can for most purposes be regarded as dialects of the same tongue – with negligible exceptions like Chuvash and Yakut. The Turkic peoples deported in 1943–4 are each closely affiliated in speech with other particular members of the Turkic family. The South Crimean Tatar dialect is closest to the Turkish of Turkey and to Turkmen. North Crimean and Karachai-Balkar are close to Kazakh and Kirgiz – though the Karachai and Balkar dialects have been influenced to some extent by their Caucasian neighbours (Balkar, for instance, having the 'th' sounds).

Earlier Soviet accounts of the Crimean past are reasonably satisfactory. And again, they rightly condemn certain Russian practices such as deportation.

Volume 35 of the first edition of the *Large Soviet Encyclopaedia* (1937) has an article on the 'Crimean ASSR'. It describes the conquest of the area by the Tatars from previous nomads in the thirteenth century, their setting up of their own Khanate independent of the Golden Horde in 1425, and the influence on it of 'western Italian culture' from the Genoese settlements. The period of Russian attempts on the country follows, with their success in 1783. After that land was given to palace favourites and 'heavy colonial oppression' caused mass emigration, so that 300,000 Tatars had already gone by 1790. In the nineteenth century Russification and further 'dislodging' of the Tatars from the Crimea took place as a result of 'the anti-Tatar policy of the colonizers':

In the autumn of 1854 there followed a decree of the Minister of War to the effect that 'the Emperor has ordered all inhabitants of the Muslim faith living in coastal areas to be removed from the coast into inland provinces'. This measure, which was carried out in connection with the Crimean War from considerations, as it were, of a military character, was needed by the Tsarist Government to enable it to seize the richest lands on the southern coast of the Crimea. The persecution and brutalities initiated against the Tatars by the military authorities because of their alleged acts of espionage, turned this transfer of population into a wholesale flight.

In 1860–2, 231,177 Tatars emigrated, and Alexander II is condemned for approving this. Finally the Russian government, to prevent the whole area becoming a desert before Russians could be found to inhabit it, stopped further emigration. But a new wave of peasants who had been robbed of their land started to leave the country in the nineties. 'Inequality', 'national antagonism' and 'the moral and spiritual degradation of the oppressed people' are spoken of. And revolts, starting in 1808, are referred to.

In the nineteenth century Panturk feelings among the 'bourgeois intelligentsia' are mentioned, increasing greatly in the 1914 war when they became so widespread that 'the great influence of bourgeois nationalists among the broad Tatar masses contributed to the suppression of class contradictions'. In 1917 the 'nationalist-Tatar counter-revolution' with its party, the Milli Firka, took power, calling an all-Crimean Muslim Congress in Simferopol on 25 March. The main strength of the revolution in the Crimea is stated to have been the workers of Sevastopol, i.e. Russians. After the Bolshevik Revolution, the Tatar nationalists summoned a Kurultai in Bakhchisarai on 10 September 1917 and set up a government with its own armed forces. Soviet power was established by Russian arms by February 1918, though it is admitted that 'the Crimean village' was not represented in the revolutionary committee.

Another Soviet account makes the role of Russian arms clearer still:

> Tatar bourgeois nationalists, having already united in the period of the February Revolution in the Milli Firka (national party), formed, in December 1917, their own 'national government' – the bourgeois nationalists' parliament (Kurultai) in Bakhchisarai. Here the struggle for the power of the Soviets was prolonged and bitter. The workers of Sevastopol and the revolutionary sailors of the Black Sea Fleet played a decisive role in this struggle. At the beginning

of January 1918, the armies of the Kurultai were destroyed by revolutionary detachments and the power of the Soviets was established in Simferopol and, after Simferopol, throughout the Crimean Isthmus as well.[7]

The *Encyclopaedia* goes on to speak of 'nationalist agitation' and kulak risings brought about by the Milli Firka. When the Germans approached, the nationalists rose and again drove out the Communists. The German occupation, after a number of Soviet inroads, was followed by that of the White Army under Denikin which suppressed the nationalist 'directory'. In November 1920, the Soviets finally reconquered the country. And on 18 October 1921 Lenin signed a decree setting up a Crimean ASSR.

The *Encyclopaedia* goes on to say that the Milli Firka continued to resist, sowing 'national discord'. Nationalist feeling in the Communist party itself now became acute, as well as 'armed struggle in the form of banditism'. In 1928 the Central Committee liquidated 'Veli Ibrahimism' – followers of the Crimean Communist President of the Republic, who was shot with many of his supporters about that time. There then took place the final 'uprooting of kulak-nationalist elements' from the Party. In 1936 the Party had 16,252 members of whom 2,257 were Tatars.

It is scarcely necessary to quote Soviet statements about the satisfactory position the Crimean Tatars had now attained. These resemble in every respect those made for all the other minorities of the USSR, and repeat almost word for word what has already been quoted about the Chechens. Their votes in Soviet elections were adequately unanimous and the speeches of their leaders full of loyalty and thanks to the regime.

As for Crimean Tatar culture, the first edition of the *Large Soviet Encyclopaedia* speaks of 'talented writers grown up in the struggle with remnants of bourgeois nationalism'. But they were in fact renowned for a lively folk literature, much of it politically unobjectionable. As late as 1940 a Russian translation of some of these tales was produced in Moscow.

In World War II their country was, unlike Checheno-Ingushetia, actually occupied by the Germans. But reports continued to come out about Tatar bravery in anti-German partisan units and in the ranks of the Red Army. Some became Heroes of the Soviet Union. So when the decree already quoted, on the dissolution of the Chechen-Ingush and Crimean Republics, was published in 1946 it was as much a surprise in the case of the Tatars as in that of their Caucasian co-religionists.

ON THE VOLGA: THE GERMANS

There have long been a number of Germans in Russia as administrators, doctors and specialists in other fields in which trained Russians were hard to come by in early Tsarist days. But quite apart from these urbanized Germans there was a far larger element – the peasant farmers. These started to come to Russia on a big scale as a result of two decrees of Catherine the Great in 1762 and 1763 calling for foreigners to settle the empty lands from which the Russians had recently driven the Khans. Some 27,000 Germans were settled on the Volga by 1767. They were extremely successful farmers. This was partly due to their own qualities and partly to the fact that they were almost the only free peasants in a country of serfs. Though scattered to some extent over the whole arc of the Russian south-east from the Ukraine to the Urals, their great centre was in the area later to become the Volga-German ASSR.

Volume 41 of the first edition of the *Large Soviet Encyclopaedia* (1939 – i.e. only two years before the suppression of the republic) has an article on the Volga-German ASSR. It quotes the decrees of Catherine the Great which invited the Germans in and the privileges, such as exemption from military service, granted them as an incentive. It adds that in the 1880s they 'lost their privileges, suffered Russification' and underwent other oppressions. The bourgeoisie, it is stated, got control of 36·5 per cent of their land (a smaller proportion than that later acquired by the Soviet government). The German peasants, who had taken part in the Pugachev revolt in the eighteenth century, also revolted in 1905. And then:

In 1916 there was promulgated a law against 'German dominance', the application of which was also extended to cover the Volga Germans. Shortly after this preparations were put in hand for the expulsion of all Germans from the Volga area, and this was set for April 1917. The overthrow of the monarchy prevented the carrying out of this barbarous measure. When the colonists appealed to the Provisional Government to revoke this law, Kerensky only agreed 'to stay the execution of the decree'. Only the Great October Socialist Revolution, which put an end to national oppression . . . rescinded this decree.

The article goes on to say that in February 1917 the 'bourgeoisie and kulaks' of the area came to power, and that they tried to maintain an Autonomous German Province. After the October Revolution, Stalin set up a Commissariat for Volga-German Affairs and, after the defeat of an anti-Soviet rising, Lenin, on 19 October 1918, decreed the setting up of an autonomous administration – though not on the terms asked for by the local nationalists. Several German units are named by the article as having taken part in the Civil War on the Red side. The purges of the late twenties and early thirties are referred to as 'a struggle with nationalist tendencies' and it is added that the Central Committee of the All-Union Communist Party 'and the healthy core of the Party organization of the Volga Germans made it possible to defeat the nationalist-kulak tendency'. This is one of the most direct references, in the articles we are considering, to the fact that even a section of a local Party – that not included in 'the healthy core' – was 'nationalist' (i.e. opposed to Moscow domination) and pro-'kulak' (i.e. opposed to oppression of the peasantry and collectivization). It seems not unreasonable to assume that the non-Communist sections of the population were even more affected by these heresies.

The article adds that as a result of the 'carrying out of Leninist-Stalinist national policy' the area 'became a republic of flourishing socialist culture', and stresses the loyalty of the Germans equally with their prosperity in such passages as:

> During the first and second Stalin Five-Year Plans, in the periods of the all-out Socialist offensive against the capitalist

elements of town and country, the Volga-German Autonomous Soviet Socialist Republic was the foremost in carrying out collectivization in the countryside, and effectively mechanized its agriculture. Industry also developed. . . . The future development of the national economy and culture of the Volga-German Autonomous Soviet Socialist Republic, its rapid progress towards a better, still more joyous life, and towards Communism, are guaranteed by the Stalinist Constitution, by the resolute Stalinist leadership of the Central Committee of the Bolshevik Communist Party of the Soviet Union and the limitless devotion of the working people of the Volga-German Autonomous Soviet Socialist Republic to the cause of Communism.

The Volga Germans were one of the very first peoples to gain a form of autonomy in the 'German Volga Labour Commune' proclaimed in October 1918 and given the status of Autonomous Soviet Socialist Republic in February 1924. The area in 1926 had 66·4 per cent Germans in its population as against 20·4 per cent Russians and 12 per cent Ukrainians. And (a characteristic usual in Russian dependent territories though perhaps unexpected in connection with Germans) the local people formed the peasantry and the main urban population was Russian. The effect of this became even more pronounced when the capital was moved from the old German centre, Marxstadt, to the Russian town of Pokrovsk (renamed Engels) in August 1922. Eighty-six per cent of the population of the town were then Russians and Ukrainians and only 11 per cent Germans.

The collectivization campaign and the great purges hit the Volga-German Republic as hard as, though perhaps no harder than, it did other areas. The Prime Minister, Welsch, who had attacked 'nationalist and other anti-Soviet elements' in the Government and Party of the Republic in 1936, was himself arrested in 1937 together with other high officials including the President of the Republic.

After collectivization the Volga-German farms were, as we have seen, given special praise. The Soviet English daily

Moscow News said on 16 January 1939, 'These people are demonstrating to the whole world what the industrious gifted German people are capable of when they are free from the yoke of capitalism.' And in general the Volga Republic was treated as somewhat of a show place.

On 26 June 1938, in the elections in the Volga-German ASSR, 99·7 per cent of the votes were cast for the official candidates.

The deportation of the Volga Germans was an announcement of the failure of Soviet policy in the face of the ties of nationality. Nevertheless it was regarded at the time as an exceptional case. The decree, which came in September 1941, was couched in the following terms:

> According to trustworthy information received by the military authorities there are among the German population living in the Volga area thousands and tens of thousands of diversionists and spies who on a signal being given from Germany are to carry out sabotage in the area inhabited by the Germans of the Volga.
>
> None of the Germans living in the Volga area has reported to the Soviet authorities the existence of such a large number of diversionists and spies among the Volga Germans; consequently the German population of the Volga area conceals enemies of the Soviet people and of Soviet authority in its midst.
>
> In case of diversionist acts being carried out at a signal from Germany by German diversionists and spies in the Volga-German Republic or in the adjacent areas and bloodshed taking place, the Soviet Government will be obliged, according to the laws in force during the war period, to take punitive measures against the whole of the German population of the Volga.
>
> In order to avoid undesirable events of this nature and to prevent serious bloodshed, the Presidium of the Supreme Soviet of the USSR have found it necessary to transfer the whole of the German population living in the Volga area into other areas, with the promise, however, that the migrants

shall be allotted land and that they should be given assistance by the State in settling in the new areas.

For the purpose of resettlement, areas having much arable land in the Novosibirsk and Omsk provinces, the Altai territory, Kazakhstan and other neighbouring localities have been allotted.

In connection herewith the State Committee of Defence has been instructed to carry out urgently the transfer of all Germans of the Volga and to allot to the Germans of the Volga who are being transferred lands and domains in the new areas.

President of the Presidium of the Supreme Soviet of the USSR:

(Signed)   M. KALININ.

Secretary of the Presidium of the Supreme Soviet of the USSR:

(Signed)   A. GORKIN.

Moscow: Kremlin, 28 August 1941.

(*Bulletin of the Supreme Soviet of the USSR,*
No. 38, 2 September 1941.)

A later decree (of 7 September 1941) divided the Volga German territory – fifteen raions going to the Saratov and seven to the Stalingrad provinces.[8]

Thus a people whose 'devotion to Communism' had been publicly asserted and who had demonstrated their unanimity in Soviet elections were submitted to a fate officially described as 'barbarous' when threatened by the Tsars.

4

HOW MANY WENT?

THE total numbers deported in these operations can only be estimated, for a variety of reasons. A basic minimum figure on which we can work can, indeed, be obtained easily enough. The Soviet census of 1939 gives the following figures:

Chechens	407,690
Ingushi	92,074
Karachai	75,737
Balkars	42,666
Kalmyks	134,271

The Volga Germans and Crimean Tatars are not listed. But the *Large Soviet Encyclopaedia* gives them as percentages of the population of their ASSRs, as follows:

Volga Germans
66·4% of
  576,000   - 382,000 (1933)
(*L.S.E.*, Vol. 41,
  1st edition)

This is kept in round numbers as the original is a Soviet estimate in round numbers, not a census figure.
(The total population of the Republic in 1939 was 605,542.)

Crimean Tatars
23·1% of
  875,100   - 202,000 (1936)
(*L.S.E.*, Vol. 35,
  1st edition)

(The total population was 1,126,824 in 1939, which implies that the 1936 estimate is low.)

The Meskhetians are not listed. But the 1926 Census gives 137,921 'Turks' in Georgia (a figure which omits the Kemshins and Kurds). This too is a low and early figure, but for the moment we may take it for a minimum total of 1,474,359.

By the time of the deportations the first five nations should, at their usual rates of increase, have gone up by about 60,000 souls. This is, indeed, based on their gains in the 1926–39 period (see p. 160), whereas half of the 1939–43/4 period was in war-time. But equally, half the 1926–39 years were times of terror or of famine which, in general, produced about equal casualties in the USSR.

As to the Volga Germans and Crimean Tatars, we are of course dealing with estimates only, and these were out by as much as 15 per cent in the case of other nations. However, accepting these, we must in any case add 30,000 to 40,000 to the Crimeans, if their increase was at the average Tatar rate, and about 30,000 to the Volga Germans, assuming the average rate for Soviet Germans as a whole. In Meskhetia the 'Turks' should have increased to about 180,000 in the period, and we may conservatively add 20,000 for the three lesser groups in their community.

This gives a grand total of approximately 1,650,000.

If the view is taken that the war was, after all, more destructive than the peace-time troubles, at least in these particular areas, and we go to the length of allowing no net increase at all in the period 1941–3/4, we must reduce the North Caucasian nations by some 30,000; the Crimeans by about 12,000; and the Meskhetians by 7,000, which would bring our grand total down to 1,600,000. This round number, of over $1\frac{1}{2}$ million souls, may perhaps be taken as a reckoning, conservative enough to be acceptable to everybody, of those despatched into exile in General Serov's cattle-trucks in a particular set of deportation operations distinguished from others of the sort in a single respect – that this time it was whole peoples that were being sent into oblivion.

Our figures do not, it should be noted, include the large number of Germans outside the Volga Republic. The total number of Germans in the USSR was 1,423,000 on the eve of the war. Some of them were in Soviet Asian settlements already, but those in the European parts of the USSR were deported

c

together with their fellow nationals on the Volga, and their various National Districts (17 in all) were abolished in the same way as the Volga Republic. It is difficult to estimate the numbers involved, for most of these Districts were in the Ukraine, and many were overrun by the Nazis before the Soviet authorities could take action. On their withdrawal the Nazis evacuated all Germans. It has been estimated that the Russians succeeded in deporting about 200,000 from the Ukraine, the Crimea and the North Caucasus' and we may conservatively reckon the same number again from other parts of Russia.

These non-Volga Germans are, however, not strictly speaking our concern in this book, any more than the million-odd Balts and the similar number of Ukrainian deportees who followed them.

The size of the depopulated territories was approximately 62,000 square miles, that is, more than seventeen times the area of the island of Cyprus; or more than the size of Czechoslovakia and Albania together.

It was divided as follows:

Chechen-Ingush ASSR - - - - -	6,060
Crimean ASSR - - - - - -	10,036
Karbardine-Balkar ASSR: estimate of Balkar area (total 4,747) - - - - - -	950
Kalmyk ASSR - - - - - -	28,641
Volga-German ASSR - - - - -	10,503
Karachai AP - - - - - -	3,831
Meskhetia (estimate) - - - - -	2,000
	62,021

European settlers, mainly Russian, took the land.

5

THE MEMORY HOLE

In this chapter we examine Soviet publications of the time for information about the deportations and deported nations. The results are extraordinary, not to say sinister, by the standards prevailing in the non-Communist world. Direct information about anything involved – even the past existence of these peoples – was, in fact, almost totally suppressed. Inspection of Soviet documents rapidly becomes a piece of detective work, a search for indirect clues, rather than normal reference activity.

With very few exceptions, which we will deal with, nothing was said about the nations concerned for a period of about ten years. Apart from the Chechen-Ingush and Crimean decree published in *Izvestia* in June 1946, they seem simply to have disappeared from the category of admitted entities. They are ignored almost as if they had never been – in some cases, exactly as if they had never been. There are precedents for this occurring in the case of individuals in the USSR: men like Kossior and Eikhe, or Meyerhold and Babel, were for decades what George Orwell christened 'unpersons'. The 'unnation' was a new phenomenon.

When the decree on the suppression of the Chechen-Ingush and Crimean Republics became known in 1946, and those interested began to examine the maps which then appeared giving the new territorial arrangements, they noticed that certain other national areas had disappeared too. Moreover, as Kolarz points out,[1] if simple transfer of population had been all that was implied, 'it would have been conceivable for the Volga-German Republic to be resurrected on the banks of the Ob, Irtysh or Yenisei', and similarly with the other nations. No such republics were shown.

What the maps did show was that the Volga-German, Chechen-Ingush, Crimean and Kalmyk Republics and the Karachai Autonomous Province had disappeared, and that the Kabardine-Balkar Republic now existed only in truncated form as the Kabardine ASSR simply. Except for the Crimea, which now appeared as the Crimean Province, the missing autonomous units had all been partitioned.*

In most cases, as we shall see, the place names in the old local languages had also gone, being replaced by new Russian ones.

The deduction from this (and other material we will consider later) was that the Kalmyks, Karachai and Balkars had been deported too. This was true, but it was to receive no official confirmation until 1957.

A look at the political and physical map shows that in the case of the Karachai, Balkars, Ingushi and Chechens the territorial rearrangements were rather peculiar. As we have said, the main Karachai and Balkar regions to the north and east of Mount Elbrus respectively were both annexed to Georgia which also obtained a large area of the south part of the former Chechen-Ingush Republic. An important gain was also made by the North Ossetian Autonomous Republic.

This provides some insight into the rating of the nations by the Soviet government. Georgia, Stalin's (and Beria's) home republic, was inordinately favoured. Moreover its spread right

---

* The Volga-German ASSR went mainly to the Saratov Province, with the southern strip going to the Stalingrad Province.

The Kalmyk ASSR was mainly incorporated in a new Astrakhan Province, with smaller areas handed over to the Stalingrad Province, the Rostov Province and the Stavropol Territory.

The Karachai Autonomous Province was largely ceded to the Georgian SSR, with smaller areas going to the Krasnodar Territory, the Cherkess Autonomous Province and the Stavropol Territory.

The Upper Baksan Valley, the main Balkar area, went to Georgia, while the rest of Balkaria remained in the newly renamed Kabardine ASSR.

The Chechen-Ingush ASSR was mainly incorporated in a new Grozny Province, with a western strip consisting of most of Ingushetia going to the North Ossetian ASSR, an eastern area, with Shamil's old capital Vedeno, handed over to the Daghestan ASSR, and the mountainous southern portion ceded to the Georgian SSR.

across the dividing line of the main chain of the Caucasus was unprecedented. In fact the division of the Ossetian nation into two separate administrative areas – the North Ossetian ASSR and the South Ossetian Autonomous Province (the latter forming part of Georgia) had been justified on the grounds of the physical division produced by the mountains.

Administrative Divisions in the North Caucasus 1945

That the North Ossetian Republic was given an increase in territory over an area hitherto unconnected with it, while the Kabardines were only allotted part of the Balkar area previously administered from their own capital, Nalchik, also tends to confirm that the Kabardines were at this time less well thought of than the Ossetians. It is perhaps relevant that the Central Committee decree of 10 February 1948, criticizing Muradeli's opera *The Great Friendship*, while condemning the Chechens and Ingushi for their actions in the 1917 Revolution finds it necessary to put forward only the Ossetians and Georgians as reputable nations (see p. 80).

It was with interest that new editions of other Soviet reference books were looked at, for what further information they might now give about the deported nations. It was found that they now said – nothing at all. Not only was each nation's present obliterated, but its past as well. Except in very occasional circumstances their names had become almost literally unspeakable. This silence, only practicable in a land with a totalitarian state organization, was a strong indication of the regime's view of truth. It also gave little reason to suppose that the Chechens, the Kalmyks and the others were likely to be receiving good treatment.

The sources that can be checked for such negative evidence are plainly of rather a special nature. If there happened to be no book published or article written in Britain for a number of years about, say, the Falkland Isles, it might be odd, but would scarcely prove anything. But there are certain publications which must ordinarily deal with all areas and peoples and from which their omission is significant. In the first place compilations such as encyclopaedias come to mind. And a good deal of the most striking information comes from the second edition of the *Large Soviet Encyclopaedia*.

This important orthodox and official compilation has so far had two editions. The volumes appear (apart from certain irregularities) one by one in alphabetical order. The last volume of the first edition came out in 1948. The second edition, in larger volumes, then started to come out in 1949 and was completed, with its fifty-first volume, in 1958.

Before we look at the second edition of the *Encyclopaedia* we can refer to the last volumes of the first edition which came out after the deportations. There are only a few of them, one being Volume 50, which has an article on the North Ossetian Autonomous Republic. It appeared in September 1944, and showed on the accompanying sketch map that the republic was bounded by the Kabardine Republic (not the Kabardine-Balkar Republic) and the Grozny Province (not the Chechen-Ingush Republic). It seems that no one in the West noticed this at the time. And in the same volume it was found possible to assert, in a short article on the North Caucasus, that in the war 'The mountain nationalities of the North Caucasus had displayed outstanding heroism both in the Red Army and in extensive partisan fighting.'

The composite volume of the first edition on *The U.S.S.R.* came out in October 1947. The names of the abolished republics and deported peoples are not given either in lists or on maps. On p. 60 the population of the USSR is listed by 'national composition', within the 1939 boundaries. The 20,000 Assyrians are listed; 88,000 Adygei and 164,000 Kabardines are noted. The number of Greeks in the USSR is given as 285,900. But none of the then deported nations is named, unless indeed they are under 'others' of whom there are 2,983,000. The only oblique hint at a missing people, the Balkars, is given in the population of the Kabardine Republic as of 1933, which is said to have been 60 per cent Kabardine and 10·7 per cent Russian, simply.

We have already quoted largely from the first edition, and it will now be seen how useful a comparison has thus been provided with what was not given in the second edition. For the existence of the first edition provides a way of checking the sort of space and treatment given to a nation or area in the ordinary way – a control, as the scientists say.

The new edition is most attractively produced and the scientific and certain other articles are very well done. It is a thorough publication, and is printed in 300,000 copies. The importance attached to it by the Soviet authorities, as an expression of right-mindedness, is very great, as various incidents show. The fact that the volume containing the article on Stalin, No. 40, was delayed for over a year, until every other succeeding volume had already been produced, shows that decisions on these matters are not made lightly nor on a low level. In two cases special measures of a rather startling kind have been taken: the sending round to subscribers of instructions to remove certain pages and replace them with others supplied. The first dealt with the excision of a long article on Beria and its replacement by photographs of the Bering Sea and an article on an eighteenth-century figure called Berggolz, and the second, similarly, ordered the removal of the article on the purged Chinese Communist leader, Kao Kang (Gao Gang in Russian), and its replacement by articles on various towns in Africa and elsewhere beginning with the relevant letter.

It will be seen from the dates that the greater bulk of the second edition of the *Encyclopaedia* had come out before there was any question of the 1957 rehabilitations of deported nations, but that some of the later volumes followed that announcement: thus the treatment of Balkars, Kalmyks or Ingushi might be expected to be different from that of Chechens – *Ch* being a late letter in the Russian alphabet.

As we shall see, the first slight signs of any recognition of the existence of the deported peoples began to appear in 1955. But the first fairly definite indication that restoration was intended for the majority of them came in Khrushchev's Secret Speech. This was made in February 1956. The last volume to come out before that speech was Volume 38, taking things as far as *SIG*.

By this time the bulk of the deportees and their areas could have been covered. The Balkars, Karachai, Kalmyks and Ingushi, as races, and the Germans too; the Karachai Autonomous Province, the Kalmyk Autonomous Soviet Socialist Republic, the Kabardine-Balkar Autonomous Soviet Socialist Republic, the Crimean Autonomous Soviet Socialist Republic, the Volga-German Autonomous Soviet Socialist Republic, as political units, and the Caucasus as a historical and ethnic area of study, should have had individual articles, as in the first edition, giving some information about the nations.

The second edition (except in a special supplementary Volume 51, published in 1958) contains no articles at all on the Balkars, the Ingushi, the Kalmyks, the Kalmyk ASSR, the Karachai, the Karachai Autonomous Province or the Volga-German Republic.

Instead of an article on the Kabardine-Balkar ASSR, there is one on the Kabardine ASSR (in Volume 19). It runs to thirteen and a half pages. There is no mention of the Balkars. The population is said to be mainly Kabardine, with 40 per cent Russian and Ukrainian. A misrepresentation of the facts occurs, as the republic is referred to as simply 'Kabardine' at the time of its foundation in 1936 and in the settling of its constitution in the following year, whereas it was then actually called 'Kabardine-Balkar'. The authors do not find it out of place to add that 'the Tsarist government and local feudalists artificially aroused national enmity between the mountaineers and differences between the mountaineers and the Russian Cossacks'. Nor do they fail to conclude:

> Right from the time of the setting up of the Soviet power the peoples of Kabarda, thanks to the putting into practice of Leninist-Stalinist national policy, received every opportunity for political, economic and cultural development, in brotherly comradeship with the other nations of the USSR. . . .

The article on 'Germans' in Volume 29 (November 1954) speaks of the Germans outside Germany as existing in 'Southern Denmark, Eastern Belgium, the USA, Canada, Brazil, the Argentine and Roumania'. (It adds that by decision of the Potsdam Conference about ten million Germans were transferred to Germany from the territories of Poland, Czechoslovakia and Hungary.) Thus, though the small numbers of Germans in such countries as Brazil and Canada are mentioned, there is nothing at all on the Volga and other Germans of the USSR (who are not referred to throughout the article).

Volume 23 has an article on the Crimean Province – founded, it states, on 30 June 1944. The basic population is given as Russian and Ukrainian, and it is mentioned that there have been immigrants from the Russian provinces of Kursk, Penza, Rostov and elsewhere. There is nothing about the previously existing republic. But the Crimean past is so very important in Russian history that it seems to have not been feasible to eliminate it entirely, and Volume 23 also has an article on the Crimean Khanate which, unlike the attitude of the first edition, is treated in an extremely hostile fashion, as a centre of the slave trade and aggression in general. 'In the seventeenth century the Russian government began to prepare the annihilation of the robber Crimean Khanate.' The annexation of the area, at a time when it was supposed to be independent, is justified because anti-Russian elements are said to have wished to return to the Turkish connection. 'The unification of the Crimean Khanate to Russia in 1783 had great progressive significance in the history of the peoples of the Crimea and led to the liquidation of Turkish-Tatar aggression in the Crimea.' It also 'had great progressive significance for the social economic and cultural development of the Crimea'.

After the annexation the Tatars are not mentioned again until the time of the Revolution, when they are referred to three times: first in connection with 'stubborn resistance to the Soviet power shown by the Panturk leaders of Tatar bourgeois nationalism', secondly in that Tatar nationalists treacherously captured and shot Bolsheviks, and thirdly when 'the Germans set up a cruel colonial regime assisted by the Tatar nationalists'.

A comparison of the maps in the article on the Crimean ASSR in the first edition of the *Encyclopaedia* with those on the Crimean Province in the second edition shows a number of changes of name and the disappearance of many, though not all, of those in Tatar. For example Buyuk-Orlar becomes Oktyabrskoye (October).

In Volume 19 the article on the Caucasus has three pages on 'ethnic composition' which deals in addition with the autonomous republics and provinces of the area, by which, 'nations of a new type – socialist – were set up'. There is no reference to the deported peoples or their former administrative areas.

In the article in the same volume on the Caucasian Wars Chechniya, though not the Chechens as such, is mentioned twice – once on a historical map and once in the following sentence: 'England activized the activity of her agents among the Caucasian mountaineers, as a result of which there was a new outburst of the Muridist movement, especially in Chechniya and Daghestan.'

It might perhaps have been expected that reference, if only historical, would be made to the deported peoples in the articles on the Russian provinces in which their homelands were now included.

The provinces and territories concerned were those of

Astrakhan, Grozny, Krasnodar, Saratov, Stavropol and Stalingrad. The last two came out after the rehabilitations and, showing different circumstances, are dealt with in Chapter 13 (though it may be noted that even then the Stalingrad article contains no reference to its former Germans, who had not been rehabilitated).

In Volume 3 (May 1950) there is an article on the Astrakhan Province into which the accompanying map shows the greater part of the Kalmyk ASSR to have been incorporated. In this seven-and-a-half-page article there is no reference, historically or otherwise, to the Kalmyks. It is stated that besides population increases in the town, 'in the years of Soviet power the population has grown also in the rest of the Astrakhan Province – in the semi-desert steppe'. It is also stated that the 'majority of the population of the Astrakhan Province is Russian. The Kazakhs, Tatars and Ukrainians form significant groups.' The only hint of the past occurs when it is stated that there are two towns in the province – Astrakhan and 'Stepnoi (formerly Elista)'. Apart from Elista itself many of the village names which in the map in the first edition are of Mongol character such as Ulan-Erge, Yusta and so on are here changed to Russian ones like Krasnoi ('Red') and Trudovoi ('Labour'). Stepnoi, the new name of the capital, was Russian, and similarly the main fishing settlement Lagan turns to Kaspiiski. The article also mentions that the Astrakhan Province was set up on 27 December 1943. This fits with early unofficial statements that the Kalmyk ASSR was dissolved by a decree given that date, and published in the republic at the time of the deportation.

Similarly the article on the Grozny Province (Volume 13, June 1952) contains no reference, historical or otherwise, to the Chechens and Ingushi. Names on the map have become mainly Russianized – Krasnoarmeiskoye, Sovietskoye, Mezhdurechiye, etc. The province's date of formation is given as 22 March 1944, but, as we shall see later, it was not formed directly on the dissolution of the Chechen ASSR.

The Krasnodar Territory (Volume 23, October 1953) is shown as having annexed the upper Laba Valley from the former Karachai Autonomous Province. The population of the territory as listed includes no Karachai.

The article on the Saratov Province (Volume 38, December 1955) has no reference to Germans. The basic population is given as Russian with Ukrainian, Chuvash, Mordvin and Tatar minorities. A map shows that all the place names are now Russian, with the doubtful concession of Engels: Marxstadt becomes plain Marx.

And similarly with the articles on Georgia and North Ossetia, which had obtained parts of the suppressed autonomous territories.

Though virtually nothing thus emerges in the way of references to the deported peoples in the new accounts of their home territories, it seemed possible that they would now be dealt with in the articles on the areas to which they were deported.

In the case of the Germans, these had been officially stated to include 'the Novosibirsk and Omsk Provinces, the Altai Territory and Kazakhstan'.

The article on Novosibirsk Province in Volume 30 (December 1954) states: 'The predominant masses of the population consist of Russians' and it names 'Ukrainians and Tatars', comprising an 'insignificant percentage of the population'. The article on the Omsk Province in Volume 31 (February 1955) says, 'The basic part of the population is Russian; it is inhabited also by Ukrainians, Kazakhs, Tatars and others.'

The Altai Territory article in Volume 2 (March 1950) says that 'The predominant mass of the population' is Russian, the next in number Ukrainians, and 'in no great number Chuvashes and Kazakhs', and 'in the High-Altai Autonomous Province the basic population consists of Altais'. The article on the High-Altai Autonomous Province in Volume 12 (May 1952) speaks simply of a basic population of Russians and Altais.

It was later made clear that not only Germans, but also a number of the other deported nationalities, had been sent to Kazakhstan and Kirgizia. For instance (see pp. 141–3) Chechen and Ingush newspapers began to appear in these territories in 1955–6. However the articles on the Kazakh and Kirgiz SSRs in the second edition of the *Large Soviet Encyclopaedia* make no references to these peoples. In Volume 19, passed for publication on 16 June 1953, the article on Kazakhstan says 'the basic population is Kazakh, forming with Russians 80 per cent of the whole population of the republic. In Kazakhstan are also settled Ukrainians, Uzbeks, Uigurs, Dungans, Tatars, Koreans,* Karakalpaks, etc.' The Kazakhs, it adds, live 'in close comradeship with the Russian, Ukrainian and other bordering nations'. Similarly in Volume 21, passed for publication on 13 June 1953, the article on Kirgizia mentions among the population the Kirgiz and eight other peoples among whom the deported ones are not named. Here too there is a reference to 'mutual trust' which prevails as a result of 'Leninist-Stalinist national policy'.

The *Encyclopaedia* shows it most bluntly. But the same nil return was made by other reference books of similar type. A few examples will show the essence of what was an almost universal phenomenon.

Economic Geography of the U.S.S.R., by N. N. Baranski (for the eighth class in Middle Schools) (Moscow, 1949), states that

> in national composition the North Caucasus is very varied. Among the basic population living here before the arrival of the Russians several tens of various nationalities may be reckoned. In their great majority they are united in autonomous republics and autonomous provinces.

It goes on to name those of the Adygei, the Cherkess, the Kabardines, the Ossetians and the Daghestanis, but no others, of those living there in pre-Russian times.

The *Soviet Atlas* No. IV for Middle Schools (On the History of the Soviet Union) falsified the position, in that it left out of its map of the administrative divisions of the Soviet Union in 1922 all the territories which were *later* suppressed. The Crimean Republic, for instance, had been founded in 1921, but is not shown.

A Geography of the U.S.S.R. by N. I. Lyalikov (Moscow, 1955), described as for teachers, has in its chapter on the Caucasus a section on 'population' in which the offending nations are

---

* These are the Koreans deported from the Vladivostok border area in the thirties – the first operation of this sort.

not mentioned even historically. The Tsarist campaigns are said to have been against simply 'the mountaineers'. 'Bourgeois-nationalism' during the Civil War is referred to. And non-deported races like the Kabardines, Circassians and the Ossetians are listed. In the section on national autonomy the republics and areas listed do not include those suppressed earlier. Such was the general run of things.

The constitutional formalities were observed in the February 1947 session of the Supreme Soviet of the USSR, when, on the basis of a speech by Vyshinsky, Article 22 of the Constitution was amended to list the administrative divisions of the country, omitting the suppressed republics. The earlier text was not referred to.

There was a further unmistakable indication that the deportees had lost all civil rights. Not only were no new auto-nomous regions erected for them, but their previous repre-sentation in the Soviet of Nationalities of the Supreme Soviet, which supposedly guards the interests of the minorities, was suppressed. *Izvestia* of 15 June 1950 lists the nationalities represented there after the 1950 elections. There is none from the nations in question. In the Soviet of Nationalities elected in 1937 they had the following numbers: Volga Germans 10; Kalmyks 9; Chechens 5; Balkars 4; Karachai 3; Ingushi 1. (The Crimean representation was not clearly differentiated, but seems to have been 5 or 6.)

The administrative reference books, like the maps, showed the new territorial arrangements.

Already, the 1942 edition of the Soviet handbook on *Admini-strative Divisions of the R.S.F.S.R.* has, in its section on admini-strative changes, in the pages dealing with the Saratov province, a list renaming former areas of the Volga-German Republic now incorporated in that province: for example Neu-Wolte has become Sverdlovo. A decree of the USSR, and three decrees of the RSFSR, are referred to as authority for the changes.

Similarly, the 1954 edition* of the handbook *U.S.S.R.:*

---

* I have seen three copies of the 1941 edition of this production. In all of them, pp. 146 and 147, where the Volga-German Republic was given, are stuck together so skilfully as to escape quite a careful look.

Territorial Administrative Divisions of the Union Republics gives the whole new layout formally, together with a list of changes of name, most of them unconnected with our subject, but a fair number being Russifications of Chechen, Tatar and Kalmyk place names. It shows Northern Ossetia increased in area from 6·2 thousand square kilometres to 9·2; Daghestan from 35·0 to 38·2, and Georgia from 69·3 to 76·4.

Changes of name are also referred to in, for example, a decree of the Presidium of the Supreme Soviet of the USSR, published on 1 February 1952, renaming twenty-nine railway stations in the Crimean Province. Russian names are substituted for the Tatar names, e.g. Taganash becomes Solenoye Ozero, Karankut becomes Otradnaya, and so on. These alterations of place-names in the Crimea continued after the Province was transferred, by a Decree of the Supreme Soviet of 19 February 1954, from the RSFSR to the Ukraine, a change probably connected with Khrushchev's policy of upgrading his old Ukrainian fief, and comparable to the cession by Stalin of some of the other de-autonomized regions to his native Georgia. In neither case, of course, did the transfer bring any benefit to the deported peoples (nor, except in a prestige sense, to the republics gaining the territory).

There were, indeed, a few residual direct references to the deportees. The previous existence of their republics was not entirely suppressed in, for instance, the collection *The Communist Party of the Soviet Union in Resolutions and Decisions*. This quotes a decree of the Council of People's Commissars of the USSR on grain cultivation. All the suppressed republics are mentioned in two tables (p. 839 and p. 846 respectively), the same as given in *Pravda*, 30 June 1937. (The volume was passed for the press on 25 September to 30 October 1953, and it also gives the fallen Beria's name in several contexts, quite apart from the decision of the Central Committee expelling him from the Party.) And there are passing references to the Chechen and Ingush languages in, for instance, *Languages of the North Caucasus and Daghestan*, published by the USSR Academy of Sciences in 1949.

In the case of the Crimeans, the distant past also was too

significant to be suppressed entirely, as we have seen already in the *Encyclopaedia*. At a 'Session on the History of the Crimea'[2] P. N. Nadinsky actually dealt with the difficulties caused by the 'persistence of survivals of capitalism in the minds of the Crimean Tatars'. And we also get such things as *Izvestia*[3] carrying a historical article on the Crimea, whose theme was the Russian historical background of the area. Russians, the writer pointed out, had been settled there long before the arrival of the Tatars in the thirteenth century.

The one highly publicized direct reference to any of the deported peoples was to a more or less historical theme, though its implications were plain. The Central Committee's decree of 10 February 1948 on 'Decadent Trends in Soviet Music', to which we have already referred, attacked the opera *The Great Friendship*, by the Georgian composer V. Muradeli, *inter alia* because

> The plot of the opera, which purports to portray the struggle for the establishment of the Soviet regime and the friendship of the peoples in the North Caucasus in the years 1918–20, is historically false and artificial. The opera creates the wrong impression that such Caucasian peoples as the Georgians and the Ossetians were at that time in enmity with the Russian people, which is historically false, inasmuch as it was the Ingushi and the Chechens who were during that period the obstacle to the establishment of the friendship of the peoples of the North Caucasus.[4]

This statement, which contradicted all previous Soviet historical views, seemed to have no purpose but to brand the Chechens and Ingushi as incurable recidivists on the one hand, and on the other to make it clear that nothing favourable about them, however true, would be permitted on the part of any Soviet writer. The branding of the whole of the past life of an individual who had strayed was old Stalinist practice, as in the cases of Trotsky and Bukharin. But the application of the principle to the past of whole nations was a new refinement in the rewriting of history.

A similar line was taken in the following years in professional circles. Among historians blamed for various ideological faults in 1949 was Professor I. M. Razgon, severely criticized for 'distorting' the history of the revolution in the North Caucasus. In a book published in 1941[5] he had depicted the Ingushi and Chechens as 'revolutionary'. At that time he presumably did not foresee that these nations would turn out to be the wrong people to praise. This manipulation of history was soon extended to an earlier period still, when, as we shall see later, the wars of the mountaineers against the Tsars came to be denounced.

A straightforward statement on the deportations themselves appears in a law book published in 1948. It may not be the only one, but such are certainly most rare. It is revealing:

> In the background of the patriotic enthusiasm which inflamed the nations of the Soviet country united against the common enemy . . . there stand out strangely the monstrous, criminal and treacherous acts of some small backward nations which gave support to the enemy in the expectation of receiving 'privileges' from him at the expense of the other nations of the Soviet Union. These acts called for necessary and extraordinary measures by the Soviet State in the interests of the USSR as a whole and of all the Soviet nations who remained faithful to their Fatherland and to freedom; these measures consisted in the liquidation of certain autonomous republics of the RSFSR (for instance, the Autonomous Republic of the Volga Germans, the Crimean Autonomous Republic, and the Chechen-Ingush Autonomous Republic).[6]

The 'for instance' seems carefully phrased: only the liquidations made public are named, but there is latitude for the possibility of others having taken place. Here, too, the assertion is made flatly that 'nations' and not just elements among them gave support to the Germans. The privileges sought are not stated. Nor is the fact that the nations were the majority of those small enough to deport which had been reached by the Germans.

Another law book lays down the motives and methods of carrying out 'resettlement' for security purposes. Whether based on the deportations or not, it certainly defines *ex post facto* the Soviet legal, or at least actual, position:

> Resettlement is carried out by the state organs of the USSR:
> (1) for the purpose of realizing measures connected with state security and defence of state frontiers and
> (2) for the purpose of acquiring lands for agricultural production.
> The first function is carried out by the organs of state security.[7]

Such are the official statements, few and incomplete, in which information about the nations and the Soviet attitude to them could be read or deduced. In retrospect, indeed, certain earlier statements gradually began to reveal their significance. For instance Ivan Serov was awarded the Order of Suvorov, First Class, reserved for major victories in the field, on 9 March 1944 – that is, immediately after the largest of his deportation operations, that of the Chechen-Ingush. (He was later made a Hero of the Soviet Union and received a number of other orders.)

On the whole, therefore, we see that almost nothing was publicly stated about the deported nations after they had gone into penal exile, except by implication. No news of their lives, or even their location, was allowed to be printed for ten years.

It is not easy to understand the motives for the publication of the Chechen-Ingush and Crimean decree, on the one hand, and the silence about the other nations on the other. We may perhaps take it that the single official announcement (which presumably became widely known in other minority territories – including areas like Lithuania where a partisan struggle was still being waged) was intended as a sharp reminder to the smaller Soviet nations. The silence apart from this single brief statement prevented any campaign against the deportations in the free world having a series of incidents to feed on. It was not, of course, that the Kalmyk, Karachai and Balkar deportations could be kept secret indefinitely, nor that fuller accounts of the Chechen-Ingush and Crimean affairs would not inevitably become available from scattered defectors. Yet single voices, able to tell usually only of events some years old, did not provide the stream of news items which significant foreign interest needs to build up. Perhaps the brutal warning of the published decree had its intended effect internally. Certainly the studied silence which followed it, combined with the impermeability of the Soviet Union to investigation by free journalists, paid the Soviet leaders – up to a point.

6

THE TRIAL OF SHAMIL

THE only aspect of the whole business about which a good deal was written in the Soviet Union was in a historical polemic, starting in 1950, about what had hitherto been regarded as the proudest period in the history of the North Caucasus – the resistance to Tsarism led by Shamil. This retrospective purge of the Imam and his followers is of great significance in what it showed, and often asserted overtly, about Soviet nationality policy, and incidentally throws so much light on Soviet controversial methods that it is worth looking at at some length.

In reality Shamil's main strength lay in Chechniya. But his movement covered a wide and multinational area of the North Caucasus, and he himself was an Avar from Daghestan. It was thus possible to attack him and his 'cult' without actual reference to the Chechens. And they are seldom if ever mentioned in the polemics, which either refer to 'the mountaineers' in general, or stick in a marked manner to references to Daghestani, or even Azerbaidzhani, support for (or more usually oppression by) the Imam. He is treated, in fact, largely as the worst and most typical case of anti-Russian nationalism, and the habit of respecting him as a bourgeois-nationalist deviation of the worst sort. At the same time, it should be noted, lesser campaigns were being directed against smaller nuisances of nationalist history, like the Kazakh leader Kenesari Kasymov. In any case one would hardly be far wrong in regarding the Shamil tradition as exactly what had inspired the Chechens to resistance to Soviet rule, or in feeling that the Soviet rulers understood this point.

Even his contemporary opponents granted many admirable qualities to the Caucasian leader. Tolstoy, whose Caucasian tales must be one of the most remarkable feats of insight into the feelings and thought of a foreign people ever to have been performed, has a description of Shamil in Chapter 19 of his *Hadji Murad*. This is in 1852, after an unsuccessful campaign, when the Imam is shown exhausted by his difficulties, yet dignified and commanding. It is a restrained and quite unsentimental account, but the effect is a strong one, and probably as close to a reconstruction of the Caucasian hero as we are likely to see.

Tolstoy's account is more objective than that of Russians of the time less able to look at things *sub specie aeternitatis*. But still, his story was printed freely under the Tsars. The Tsarist regime had, too, spared the life of its most intransigent opponent when he was finally captured. And other Russian accounts give Shamil at least a certain admiration, however reluctant. It was not until 1950 that the successors of the Tsars retrospectively proved (with 'documents') just how unforgivably criminal the Imam's resistance had been.

At first Soviet publications had been wholly enthusiastic about Shamil. In its article on Shamil the first edition of the *Large Soviet Encyclopaedia* (Volume 61, 1934), says:

> The movement was aroused by the colonial policy of Russia, which robbed the basic population of their forests, tore away the best parts of their land for Cossack colonization, and in every way supported and sustained the despotism of the local feudalists. The popular rising carried out against Russia and against the local ruling strata was basically anti-feudal.

The article goes on to say that the social aims of the insurgents were disguised in religious forms, and that the rising was carried on as a struggle against the Russians on the one hand and for the Shariya – Moslem law – on the other. It quotes Engels on the religious forms taken by the peasant risings in the Middle Ages, of which he had said 'from the equality of the sons of God they deduced civil equality'. The article adds, 'the idea of equality lay at the foundation of the interpretation of Mohammedan theology by the popular masses of the Caucasus insurgent movement'. The Murid Kurali-Magoma is quoted as saying 'equality must exist among all Mohammedans'.

On Shamil himself it says that he showed the qualities of 'an outstanding political leader and a fine war chief', that he had 'enormous authority' among the masses and showed extraordinary personal heroism and skill, becoming a popular legend. His general ideas, and the religious-political organization he established to put them into practice, produced an extraordinary unity even in the 'multi-racial and multi-lingual Caucasus', which was united 'as one in the direct struggle against the colonial policy of Tsarism for its national liberation'. The article quotes Marx's dictum that Shamil was 'a great democrat'.

Even during the war against the Germans some use was made of the Shamil tradition. There was talk at the outset of the Caucasian mullahs proclaiming a Gazava – holy war – against the invaders. And Shamil's own name came in too. For instance the Daghestanis were reported as contributing 25,000,000 roubles to equip a tank column called 'Shamil'.[1]

Even after the deportations it was for a time possible for Soviet historians to describe events of past history from the anti-colonialist point of view. In A. M. Pankratova's *History of the U.S.S.R.*[2] there is still the old line on Shamil.

> Shamil was an outstanding political leader and military commander. . . . Shamil was a gifted organizer of the state structure of the mountaineers and of their armed struggle against the Tsarist colonizers. . . . The power of the beys and khans was liquidated everywhere. . . . Shamil emancipated a considerable number of slaves. . . . Shamil's action was directed at that time not only against Tsarism but also against the local feudal lords and was democratic and progressive.

On the war itself she mentions that in 1859 most of the villages of the Western Caucasus 'were burned and pillaged' and that, between 1858 and 1864, 400,000 mountaineers were deported from the Caucasus and their lands resettled with Russians.

Sporadic though unsupported attacks on Shamil were made as early as 1947,[3] but in 1950 there came a total and officially dictated reversal of the previous view. Shamil was depicted for the first time as a pure reactionary, and an agent of foreign imperialism. It was first announced that the Stalin Prize awarded only the previous year to *From the History of Social and Philosophical Thought in Azerbaidzhan in the Nineteenth Century*, by Geidar Guseinov (Baku, 1949), had been withdrawn on account of his attitude to Shamil.

Pravda and *Izvestia*, on 14 May 1950, reported that the Stalin Prize Committee 'in connection with the proposals of public organizations in Azerbaidzhan' discussed the question of Geidar Guseinov's book. It was now stated to be written 'from an incorrect political and theoretical standpoint' and particularly distorted the character of the Muridists, depicting them as progressive, democratic and national-liberationist. The author had said that Shamil 'in every possible way tried to help the Azerbaidzhanian peasants in their struggle against Tsarism' and had agreed with a bourgeois historian that Shamil 'is a hero and maker of heroes' and 'chosen of the people'. This evaluation was anti-Marxist and contradicted historical fact, because the movement was really reactionary and nationalist and 'in the service of British capitalism and the Turkish Sultan'. The Commission added, 'the idealization of Muridism in G. Guseinov's book is in essence a reflection of bourgeois-nationalist deviation and should be strongly condemned'. The nomination for the prize was withdrawn and Guseinov committed suicide to avoid arrest.[4]

This sudden highly official pronouncement was followed by a great campaign to clean up Soviet historiography from the errors into which it had fallen on the subject. Daniyalov, the Party secretary in Daghestan, repudiated Shamil. But the major statement, in the Party's theoretical organ, *Bolshevik* (No. 13, July 1950), was made by Bagirov, Party Secretary in Azerbaidzhan, and later to be shot as Beria's agent.

This 15,000-word article, 'The Problem of the Character of the Movement of Muridism and Shamil,' which was cited continually in other periodicals in the campaign that followed, is a set piece of Stalinist methods, and deserves quoting at length:

Lenin and Stalin teach that not every national movement is a progressive liberation movement. There are cases when national movements have a reactionary character, clash with the interests of development of the revolutionary movement and put a brake on the development of the class self-realization of the working people.

History knows of many instances when foreign conquerors, colonizers and imperialists have organized and supported various movements, giving them a national or religious character, with the aims of usurpation in their struggle against their rivals.

It is necessary to consider in this light and to criticize the mistaken conception, which has wide circulation in our Soviet historical literature, of the allegedly progressive, liberating character of the movement of Muridism and Shamil in the first half of the nineteenth century . . . .

In the works of many Soviet historians (S. K. Bushuev, R. M. Magomedov, M. Krovyakov and others), in the articles in the *Large Soviet Encyclopaedia*, in history textbooks for schools and higher educational institutions, Muridism and the Shamil movement are considered a liberating and progressive phenomenon. This anti-Marxist assessment of the movement of Muridism and Shamil found its reflection in the discussion 'On the Historical Essence of Caucasian Muridism', held in 1947 by the History Institute of the USSR Academy of Sciences . . . .

In order correctly to assess the movement of Muridism and Shamil, it is necessary to know that Muridism is a religious trend, one of the reactionary and warlike manifestations of Islam. As is well known, Islam arose in the seventh century in the feudal-merchant aristocracy which used Islam to unite the Arab tribes and to establish its power . . . .

Muridism, the most warlike tendency in Islam, carried to extreme limits the religious intolerance expressed in the idea of a 'holy war' against the 'infidels'. From extant facts and documents it is evident that in implanting Muridism in the Caucasus the Turks and the British based their chief calculations on this aspect of Muridism – its intolerance of 'infidels' . . . .

Shamil from the very beginning, like his predecessors, was closely linked with Turkey and acted in her interests . . . .

For a loyal attitude to Russia, for the slightest suspicion of ties with the Russians, Shamil destroyed even the people of his own faith – Moslems. Shamil and his predecessors, Kazi Muhammed and Gamzat Bek, dealt mercilessly with the population of villages and those individuals who refused to take part in the struggle against Russia . . . .

These examples provide one more proof that the Shamil movement was not one of liberation. Shamil did not consider it his task to liberate the mountain peoples. It was no accident that he did not obtain the support of the broad masses of the people of the Caucasus . . . .

Muridism was the domination of a small group of Murids, headed by the Imam, over the mass of Daghestani peasants . . . .

It is not true that Shamil destroyed all the feudal mountain lords. He persecuted and destroyed only those feudal lords who did not share his views and who opposed his activities . . . .

Apart from all the rest, Muridism and the Shamil movement sowed mistrust among the mountain tribes, hindered by that very fact their consolidation and unification and held up for many decades the economic and cultural development of the mountain peoples, which even without that were backward and ignorant. Is it really for these 'services' that certain comrades consider Shamil a national hero? How can one ignore all this numerous evidence and the facts and maintain that Shamil's 'rule' was democratic, and even go so far as to say that it was a people's republic, where the people themselves constituted the highest body of legislative power?

In such a situation it is completely beyond understanding that British lords and capitalists, who had oppressed subject peoples in their colonies by hundreds of thousands and millions, who had deprived them of their elementary human rights and privileges and sucked from them their very marrow, were supposed to help the 'national hero' Shamil, to nourish 'a special love' for the mountain nationalities and their 'liberation' movement.

In idealizing Shamil's personality not only bourgeois historians but even several of our Soviet historians go so far as to call Shamil a hero of heroes, a people's hero . . . .

What, however, is the reason that up to now the so-called Caucasian Muridism, the movement of the mountain tribes under the leadership of Shamil, has been so extolled, idealized and deceptively elucidated? It is the unscientific and uncritical attitude to this particular question; bourgeois objectivism in some and the manifestation of bourgeois nationalism in others in the elucidation of these events.

Many of our historians are in fact tied to the apron strings of bourgeois scientists, above all the British, and are held captive by a preconceived notion of Shamil as a national hero.

It is necessary to proceed to an assessment of Muridism and the movement among the mountain tribes headed by Shamil from the point of view of the general situation which was then taking shape in the south of Russia and in particular in the Caucasus.

In the eighteenth and the beginning of the nineteenth centuries the problem of their future fate faced the peoples of the Caucasus with particular acuteness. They could be swallowed up and enslaved by backward, feudal Turkey and Persia – or be annexed to Russia. Annexation to Russia was for the people of the Caucasus the only possible path for the development of their economy and culture. Inclusion in Russia created conditions for the liquidation of the economic and political parcelling out of the peoples of the Caucasus. The peoples of the Caucasus obtained security from external enemies.

Despite the arbitrary acts and cruelty of the Tsarist colonizers, the annexation of the Caucasus to Russia played a positive and progressive role for the peoples of the Caucasus . . . . The closeness to the Russian people, the joint struggle with the workers and peasants of Russia against the Tsarist autocracy and intercourse with advanced Russian culture and representatives of progressive, revolutionary social thought contributed to raising the material and spiritual culture of the peoples of the Caucasus and was a spur to the development of the revolutionary movement of the peoples of the Caucasus . . . .

The striving of advanced people in the Caucasus for union

with Russia reflected the mood of the broad masses of the people.

After the annexation of North Azerbaidzhan to Russia the Azerbaidzhanis in the ranks of the Russian Army fought heroically against their centuries-old enemies, the Turkish and Persian usurpers . . . . After this, is not the statement by G. Guseinov the basest slander on the Azerbaidzhani people, viz. 'in its struggle against the Tsarist colonial regime and the local feudal lords, the Azerbaidzhan peasantry was inspired also by the movement of Shamil'?

In the light of all that has been said, how can we understand the positions of the officials of the History Institute of the USSR Academy of Sciences, of the authors and editors of textbooks on the history of the USSR, Comrades Druzhinin, Pankratova, Zakhoder, Nechkina, Zaks and others, who idealize Muridism and distort historical truth, who extol the Muridism inspired by Russia's rivals, Turkey and Britain, and its leader Shamil?

The position of certain scientific workers and literary workers of Azerbaidzhan is also a manifestation of bourgeois nationalism: Mirza Ibrahimov, Mahmed Arif Dadash Zade and Mehti Gusein, who have published favourable reviews and appraisals of Guseinov's wrong and harmful book.

Particular responsibility for the appearance in print and the popularization of Guseinov's book is borne by the editor of this book, A. O. Makovelsky, director of the Philosophy Institute of the Azerbaidzhan Academy of Sciences, Corresponding Member of the USSR Academy of Sciences and member of the Azerbaidzhan Academy of Sciences, who, abusing his scientific and official position, has led our public into error . . . .

It is also impossible to overlook the position occupied by the USSR Union of Soviet Writers regarding Guseinov's book. The Union of Soviet Writers put forward this book for the Stalin Prize competition without having examined its content and scientific value. Incidentally, this book does not have any direct connection with the work of the Union of Writers. . . .

This extremely revealing document may thus be summarized:

(a) Some national movements are reactionary
(b) Muridism was one of these because it was anti-Russian,
pro-British and Islamic
(c) Shamil and the Murids had no popular support, were
undemocratic, and caused national dissension among
the mountaineers
(d) The Tsarist annexation of the Caucasus was progressive,
and supported by all advanced elements there
(e) Soviet historians had taken the opposite view, because
of bourgeois nationalism, bourgeois objectivism and
servility to the British
(f) They had better recant or else.

The article (which also attacked, for instance, a novel –
Shamil by P. Pavlenko, published in 1941) struck the key-note
for a major drive. It will only be worth referring to a few
examples. A decree of the Presidium of the USSR Academy of
Sciences[5] attacked a whole series of authors for 'politically
pernicious' books about Shamil, ordered institutes concerned
to hold meetings to discuss the question and to expose 'the
reactionary nationalist substance of the Muridist movement
and Shamil'; ordered the editors of *Voprosy Istorii* to publish
a series of articles attacking him; and dismissed R. M. Magomedov from the Vice-Chairmanship of the Daghestan branch
of the Academy of Sciences for his 'bourgeois-nationalist
interpretation' of the matter.

Fulfilling its instructions, *Voprosy Istorii* published a long
article on 'Sheikh Mansur and his Turkish inspirers'. Mansur
was the early Murid leader of whom Tolstoy writes that the
mountaineers held him to be a saint who had even stopped
the local blood-feud system. The magazine conceded that he
obtained the support of the 'backward mountain people' on
account of the 'colonial policy of Tsarism, the endless con-
fiscations and tribute'. The article says that Urshuma (i.e.
Mansur) 'did not justify the hopes of the common people'.
'Instead of the struggle for land, against exploitation and for the
idea of equality, Urshuma called for armed uprising against

Russia. . . . His uprising was a typical reactionary revolt directed by a foreign hand.' Many other magazines took up the affair. For instance, *History Teaching in the School*[7] attacks 'errors' on Shamil taught in the ninth grade of the secondary schools.

To support the charge that British incitement was the major factor in Shamil's movement, Soviet writers at this time made much of the travels and travel books of various Britons who had penetrated the region in the 1830s – E. Spencer, J. S. Bell, J. A. Longworth and in particular D. Urquhart, a keen champion of the North Caucasian cause who was even held partly responsible for Marx's and Engels's deviations on the subject.

The death of Stalin brought no immediate change of line on the Shamil issue. Historical works and articles published in 1954 took the old anti-Muridist view very strongly.[8]

The article already referred to on Caucasian Wars in the second edition of the *Encyclopaedia*, Volume 19 (June 1953), says, 'But the unwillingness of the mountaineers to serve as cannon fodder for the Turkish Pashas and their Anglo-French allies wrecked the calculations of the Murid leaders'. It goes on: 'The struggle of the toiling mountaineers against the despotic regime and military theocratic dictatorship of Shamil weakened the power of the Imam and foretold his total defeat.' The Muridist movement is described simply in terms of 'Mohammedan fanaticism' and Shamil himself is bluntly called 'an Anglo-Turkish agent'.

Thus for six years, three under Stalin and three under his successors, the old hero, to whom even after the deportation of his Chechens, the intellectual spokesmen of the remaining Caucasians had continued to show their attachment, was treated as pernicious and vile. In spirit he too suffered deportation. But, unlike the Chechens, he could still be spoken of, if only in a hostile fashion. And in their attitude to him the Soviet authorities demonstrated plainly what was felt about the Caucasian present as well as the Caucasian past. In effect Shamil was being blamed – *and in a sense rightly so* – for the resistance of the Chechens and others to the Soviet regime.

When the restoration of nations took place, Shamil too, as we shall see, received rehabilitation, though of a partial and grudging nature. Meanwhile he stood as the diabolical incarnation of 'bourgeois nationalism'.

7

BEHIND THE SOVIET SILENCE

FROM Soviet official information, and particularly from the blank areas now to be found in it, a reasonably clear picture could be constructed about the general nature of what happened to these peoples. But important points were missing. Not only were the destinations of the exiles not referred to, but there was little way of telling how the operations were carried out, both as a matter of police technique and from the point of view of the actual human suffering involved. On Soviet matters there were then certain readers who were not prepared to accept evidence which appeared derogatory to the regime unless it was put out by the regime itself. This was seen, for example, in the reception of Khrushchev's secret speech in 1956, which after all only confirmed and gave new detail of facts which were fairly generally known already from unofficial evidence.

The unofficial evidence on the deportations only began to emerge five or six years after the event, and then only in driblets – the odd returning Austrian POW mentioning in a newspaper interview that Chechens were to be found near his former prison camp in Karaganda; and so on. But of course Soviet evidence, though particularly unsatisfactory on the deportations, is not a model of reliability even for the pre-deportation period, and before giving some of the missing detail on the former it will be appropriate to say something more than what we have so far given from Soviet sources about the immediate background. Without this, indeed, the whole cycle of events would be incomprehensible.

We may begin with a very brief look at the post-revolutionary history of the northern Caucasus, as given by non-Soviet sources. It will have been seen already that Soviet accounts are incompatible with the deportations ever becoming necessary at all.

On 27 October 1917, a Congress of the Union of Peoples of the North Caucasus was held at Vedeno in Chechniya, Shamil's old capital, and the first point in its programme was:

> All lands and forests proclaimed Tsarist property during the conquest of the Caucasus are returned to the nations from which they have been taken away.

It also proclaimed the political union of the area.

In March 1918 the Bolsheviks formed a Terek Province People's Soviet in Pyatigorsk. The mountain peoples transferred their government to Temir-Khan-Shura (now called Buinaksk) in Daghestan. On 11 May 1918, the North Caucasian Government proclaimed independence. It signed a treaty with Turkey in June and was recognized *de facto* by the other Central Powers. Its main difficulty was lack of armaments. Southern Russia was then full of Russian Army units supporting various White or Red authorities. The North Caucasian Government obtained arms for one brigade from the German authorities in the Ukraine. And a few hundred officers and other ranks of North Caucasian race who had been serving in the Turkish Army now returned to their native land. They included Colonel-General Berkuk, a Circassian.

From the start the new government was attacked by various White and Red Russian units and from February 1919 a continuous struggle against Denikin's White Army had to be undertaken. Denikin succeeded in occupying part of Chechniya and Daghestan as early as May, but in September and October his units suffered a number of defeats. During this struggle the mountaineers were naturally thrown into alliance with the Red forces. When Denikin had been defeated, however, the 11th Red Army repeated his invasion, occupying most of the country with little opposition at first, owing to being welcomed as allies.

In 1929 to 1930 both the Chechen-Ingush and the Kabardine-Balkar populations were in revolt for most of the winter. At one time almost the whole of Balkaria was in rebel hands.

The North Caucasus suffered very severely in the great purges of the late thirties. A 'nationalist conspiracy' on the part of local leaders had been discovered in 1934. In 1937 a mass attack was made on the whole of the leading cadres of the Chechen-Ingush republic. On the night of 31 July about 14,000 were arrested, of whom a large number were executed. *Pravda* on 8 September 1937 published an article 'Bourgeois Nationalist Centre of Intrigues in Checheno-Ingushetia' which described terrorist operations by enemies of the people throughout the Republic. It added that 'hostile elements have penetrated most greatly in those districts under the direct leadership of the Chairman of the Executive Committee of the Chechen-Ingush Autonomous Soviet Socialist Republic, Gorchkhanov, the Second Secretary of the Regional Party Committee, Bakhaev, and the head of the Agitprop Section, Oknev.' The organ of the Regional Party Committee, *Groznyi Rabochii*,[1] spoke of the 'high protectors of the subversive bourgeois nationalists', naming the above mentioned and others. In October Shkiryatov arrived in Grozny and had practically the whole of the local Communist leadership arrested, including not only those already named but most of the People's Commissars and a number of writers. 137 leaders were charged with plotting to create a North Caucasian Republic under Anglo-Turkish protection. Gorchkhanov, his deputy Salamov, and others were sentenced to death and the remainder deported to labour camps. A former director of the Organizational Bureau of the Regional Committee of the Chechen Communist Party states that there were about 120,000 arrests in the North Caucasus out of a population of 3,000,000 in 1937–8, the 'General Operation' of summer 1937 producing about 100,000 of these.[2]

The Karachai and Balkars had suffered in the collectivization troubles, and about 3,000 are said to have been shot as a result of the 1929–30 rising. In 1937 the local administration was practically annihilated, and NKVD officers had to take over direct rule in the area for some time. A practice at this time which caused special resentment was the arrest of women, which had previously been avoided, even under the Tsars.

Over the same period a strong campaign against Islam had resulted in the 10,000-odd mullahs of the North Caucasus shrinking to a few hundred with a similar handful of mosques. But Mohammedanism, lacking a hierarchy, is difficult to destroy, and the mountain peoples retained their religious attachments, as in fact about the only quasi-nationalist demonstration now not totally forbidden. In this, unofficial and official accounts are at one – a thing especially objected to by the authorities being the survival, under the disguise of 'conciliation commissions', of the illegal Shariya courts, to which the Chechens voluntarily submitted their disputes.

In 1939 and 1940 there were further risings in the Caucasus. That of the Chechens was the most effective, though, as in 1930, trouble smouldered longest in the more inaccessible Balkar lands. Led by a former Communist, Hassan Izrailov, the Chechens held a considerable part of the mountain territory for some weeks and set up a provisional government. Several divisions, with air support, were concentrated against the rebels. But even after the country was largely subdued, small insurrectionary bands continued to operate in the depths of the forests.

The Kalmyks suffered severely in the collectivization drive. A decree of October 1929 on the expulsion of 'kulaks and feudalists' affected about 20,000 people, and a similar number died in the ensuing famine. As a result a Kalmyk Communist, Arash Chapchayev, openly called in 1933 for the reversal of collectivization, and there was a movement to reorganize the republic on the basis of the Mongolian People's Republic – then Sovietized but not collectivized – on the grounds that semi-nomad Kalmykia was economically comparable with the land of its co-nationals. The only result was a purge in which an estimated 5,000 perished, mainly Communist party members and intellectuals. During the same period the many lamaseries of the country were practically wiped out, and the Buddhist leaders mostly killed or driven into exile.

Crimean history, too, is inadequately covered in official accounts. On 5 May 1917, a 'National Assembly' proclaimed the autonomy of the Crimean Tatars at Simferopol. In October a Kurultai proclaimed a Crimean Democratic Republic. This was rapidly suppressed by the communists and Chlebiev, the president, was shot in February 1918.

The Hungarian Communist Bela Kun, named head of the Crimean Revolutionary Committee, was despatched to the Crimea and instituted a reign of terror, which was met by a determined partisan movement. Lenin opposed this policy and an amnesty was proclaimed. However, with the beginnings of collectivization of agriculture, the pressure on the outlying nationalities was again increased. Waves of purges struck at the national leaders. At the time of the execution of Veli Ibrahim, for 'bourgeois nationalism', some thousands of Crimean Tatars were executed or deported.

In the following years the Soviet authorities continued this policy, which was marked by the deportation of 30,000 to 40,000 Crimean Tatars during the enforcement of collectivization. A rising took place in December 1930. Successive Tatar Presidents of the Crimean Republic were purged: Mehmed Kubay for protesting during the famine of 1931–4 that 'Moscow destroys the Republic of Crimea, carries away all its natural riches without giving bread to the starving population of the peninsula'; Ilias Tarakhan, his successor, and the Chairman of the Crimean Council of People's Commissars, Ibrahim Samedin, both of whom fell to the Yezhov mass terror of 1936–1938, and were followed by a particularly large number of victims, even for those years. A 'special operation' against the Crimeans was mounted in December 1937.

In the circumstances, Soviet qualms about the loyalty of the Chechens and others became intense. The Ossetian, Colonel Tokaev, who had some access to what was being said in high political and military circles, has stated[3] that the Soviet General Staff reported in 1940 that the population of northern Caucasus would prove a handicap in case of war and recommended that 'special measures' be taken in good time. It was not, of course, until the German threat had receded that any such measures were in fact taken. The actual decision to deport the Chechens is described by Tokaev as having been taken initially at a joint meeting of the Politbureau and High Command on 11 February 1943, almost a year before it was put into effect. At this meeting,

Tokaev states that Molotov, Zhdanov, Voznesensky, Andreyev and Kosygin (then Premier of the RSFSR) urged the immediate and public liquidation of the ASSR; Mikoyan, while agreeing in principle that the Chechens should be punished, felt that such measures as deportation would be bad for the Soviet reputation; and Stalin, Voroshilov, Kaganovich, Khrushchev, Kalinin and Beria took the view that the Chechens would have to be deported eventually, but that this should be postponed until the Germans had been driven back further.

It is, of course, perfectly true that the Germans raised units from among the Chechens, as they did from most of the minority nations of the USSR – and, indeed, from the Russians themselves. Their experience seems to have been that the Chechens fought with the utmost *élan* against Soviet units but that it was impossible to make them submit to German theories of discipline.[4] German reports make it clear, too, that a Soviet writer was not exaggerating when he wrote that right from the beginning pro-Soviet partisans in the Crimea 'were deprived of the support of the local population'.[5]

For some time the only fairly complete first-hand account of the deportation operations was given by an MVD defector, Lt.-Col. Burlitsky, who took part in all of them except that of the Balkars.[6] Before Khrushchev's secret speech it was only from such accounts that the dates of several of the deportations were definitely known. Khrushchev confirmed such earlier evidence, giving in addition the Balkar date.

DATES OF DEPORTATIONS

	As given in the West 1953–6	Khrushchev's speech, February 1956
Karachai - -	October/November 1943	end of 1943
Kalmyks - -	December 1943	December 1943
Chechens and Ingushi	22 February 1944	March 1944
Balkars - -	Unknown	April 1944
Crimean Tatars -	*c.* June 1944	not mentioned
Volga Germans -	August 1941	not mentioned
Meskhetians - -	Unknown	not mentioned

A large number of Kabardines are also said to have been deported in March 1944. Since this date was given long before Khrushchev made the date of the Balkar deportation available, it seems that they went along with the smaller members of the Republic. As Walter Kolarz notes, the Kabardines exhibited much 'disloyalty' during the war with Germany,[7] and though this was not on a scale to get them deported *en bloc* as a nation considerable drafts seem to have been sent to Kazakhstan.

The NKVD concentrated for the deportation operations a large part of the military forces under their command – Border Troops, Interior Troops, Convoy Troops, and the 'Special Purpose' Troops whose main task during the war had been to remain in the rear of fighting units with the purpose of rounding up and executing them if they retreated without orders. The most notorious of these formations, the First Special Purpose Division (DON) seems to have carried out the more unpleasant tasks of deportation. The method employed was for the units to be brought into the area some weeks before the operation with the purpose of making detailed plans and familiarizing themselves with the position. When action commenced each village was surrounded by armed troops, and a number of soldiers detached to accompany the 'operational' security-police officers each detailed to round up the families in a given group of houses. In the case of the Karachai and Kalmyks the decree was formally read in the villages and each family was allowed 100 kilograms of property, including food. The inhabitants were then assembled in fields or other convenient places where they remained, often for a day and night, before the transport columns appeared to take them to the railhead. In these cases the population allotted to each regiment appears to have been in the nature of two to five thousand, which gives some idea of the size of the forces involved.

The (unpublished) decree deporting the Kalmyks is reported as having been dated 27 December 1943. The order removing Kalmyks from the army does not seem to have been put out until the following month. The Kalmyks, perhaps in accordance with their Buddhist principles, are said to have accepted their fate quietly. A number of leading Kalmyks had been able to retreat with the German armies. In 1955 about 1,300 of them belonged to the main émigré organization.[8] And they have conducted considerable and effective publicity in the countries of Asia, under their leader Dr Naminow and others.

The remaining deportations caused a considerable amount of sporadic fighting, but on the whole surprise was effected. It is extraordinary to consider the circumstances that must have prevailed for the Chechens not to have been forewarned by news of the earlier deportations, and to have been caught off guard. But all accounts agree that the NKVD units, dressed as ordinary troops, entered the republic in early February 1944, as if for manoeuvres. The size of the concentration may be judged by the fact that an entire regiment (the 95th Special Purpose Border Guards) was allotted to the single raion centre of Urus Martan. The population was assembled in the villages on the evening of 22 February 1944, to celebrate Red Army Day. They were surrounded by troops and the deportation decree was read to them by security officers. Stormy scenes ensued, in which many of the weaponless Chechens and Ingushi were shot down. The rest were rounded up and allowed to collect 50 kilograms of baggage per family (or according to some accounts 40 kilograms – in any case less than the Kalmyks). They were then driven away in trucks – mainly lease-lend Studebakers, we are told by Lt.-Col. Burlitsky, who took part in the deportation of the Chechen village of Novoselskoye. This was organized by General Serov from his headquarters at Grozny, in which town, at a special meeting, the Republic's Ministers, the Presidium of its Supreme Soviet, and the Provincial Committees of the Communist Party and the Young Communist League were put under arrest – good practice for the later trapping of Pal Maleter in Budapest.

Russian students at Grozny were sent to look after the farms in the valleys until labour could be brought in from Russia proper, and isolated mountain farms were burnt to stop use of them by 'bandits'. For a number of Chechens escaped, apart from those who for one reason or another had remained outside the villages.

The Karachai and Balkars had been the object of particularly lawless NKVD activity without a pause for several years. During the fighting in the territory in the war, there were a number of cases of whole villages being subjected to pogroms by retreating NKVD units. And on their return a good deal of punitive fighting and burning went on till order was restored, of which advantage was finally taken to deport the survivors. Even after that some resistance continued. And Karachai losses, in the actual process of deportation, are said to have been particularly heavy owing to the exceptional brutality resulting from this. As late as February 1951, it is said that numbers of Chechens and Balkars were still living an outlaw existence in the mountains.

During the winter journey of the deportees in cattle-trucks, which lasted several weeks, deaths are reported to have run as high as 50 per cent, mainly old people, but including numerous typhus victims of all ages.

The Caucasian deportees were mainly reported in Kirgizia and Kazakhstan. The few exceptions (near Sverdlovsk in European Russia and near Irkutsk in Siberia) were in special labour camps and seem to have been Chechens sent away under arrest immediately after the restoration of order in the republic and prior to the mass deportations. Those withdrawn from the Army at the time of the deportation seem to have been sent first to Kostroma in European Russia and from there, after an interval, into Central Asia. Chechens and Ingushi have been reported, often intermixed with other populations, from the area west of Frunze in Kirgizia, and from the Akmolinsk, Karaganda, Aktyubinsk, Kustanai and Petropavlovsk areas in the Kazakh SSR. There have been several accounts of a rising of Ingushi at Borovoye in the north of the Kustanai Province of Kazakhstan in the spring of 1945. It seems to have been put down with considerable bloodshed. At Krasnoyarsk about 4,000 Chechens were in penal camps. In October 1954 a successful rising in one of these camps led to a break-out and attacks on the others in which finally most of the prisoners became involved. A large proportion escaped. Mopping-up operations went on for several months, but a number of Chechens were never captured. A Soviet account of the Kolyma labour camps, too, describes a mass refusal of several hundred Chechens to work.[9]

Very little was heard of the Karachai and less of the Balkars. One of the few items published in this country about the Karachai, for instance, appears in an ex-prisoner's account of his labour-camp experiences, published here in 1954.[10] One of his fellow prisoners was a girl, Khabicheva, a Karachai from Mikoyan Shakhar who had been arrested before the deportation of her race and had been for over a year trying to find out where they had been sent. She finally discovered that they were in Kazakhstan and Kirgizia. Karachai, and possibly also Balkars, have been reported by others in the area of Kazakhstan between Dzhambul and the Kirgiz border. (It seems possible that as Turkic speakers they would be likely to be confused in other reports with 'Tatars' in general.) A Balkar location was confirmed by a member of Sir John Hunt's British Caucasian Expedition in 1958. At first an attempt was made to explain dilapidation in the Balkar area to him as the result of landslides, but finally Balkar shepherds told him of the deportations. They had been 'invited to a rally. Everyone came. When we got there troops surrounded us and the whole tribe was told that as we had co-operated with the Germans we were to be punished and deported to Central Asia.' There they lived 'beside the shores of Issyk-Kul'.[11] According to these Balkars conditions in their area of exile had, in recent years at least, been good.

There was remarkably little information on the Kalmyks. It seems in the first place that their deportation was carried out with exceptional brutality or inefficiency and that the death rate was higher in their inhospitable Siberian reception area even than that associated with the other deportees. A fair number of them seem to have ended up in the Krasnoyarsk area in Siberia.

Estimates of the total number of deaths during the journey and in the first and most difficult year of resettlement vary to some extent with the area, but most of the figures are close to two-fifths of the populations concerned, old people and children suffering most.* If we could accept this as a rough average it would imply casualties amounting to about half a million.

It will be seen that certain areas such as Karaganda received an influx of all sorts of races. Karaganda is the centre of one of the main labour-camp complexes of the Soviet Union. And with its 'free' deportee population too, it seems to have become a human dumping-ground, under police control.

Conditions reported vary between 'fair' for Chechens in the Frunze province of Kirgizia to 'very bad', little food, mud huts and so on for those in the Akmolinsk province of Kazakhstan. Even in 1955 disease 'due to under-nourishment' was said to be rampant in the Aktyubinsk province of Kazakhstan among Chechens. All reports agree that these peoples remained extremely anti-Soviet.

The work on which deportees were engaged was mainly in agriculture. Some, however, were directed to mines. And they also formed a pool for labour on canals and railway construction. The railway from Frunze to Ribachye on Lake Issyk-Kul, for instance, a difficult task involving cuttings through the gorges, was carried out almost entirely by Chechen, Ingush and Tatar labour.

The Crimean deportations followed the German evacuation of the area much more rapidly than in the other cases. The Crimea was only fully liberated in April 1944, and the Crimeans were removed in May–June – among them the members of the small pro-Soviet partisan movement, including its leader, Khaurullakh. This deportation, which seems to have been carried out with an accompaniment of much killing and brutality, was supervised by Marshal Voroshilov.

Accounts which have reached the West in the past year or so indicate that on the night of 18–19 May 1944 the Crimeans were given fifteen minutes to collect what belongings they could carry, and assembled for deportation. In some cases only five minutes were given, and no belongings or food allowed. They were mainly taken to reservations in the Urals, Kazakhstan and Uzbekistan, though they have also been noted in Yakutia,

* This estimate was published in 1960, before Academician Sakharov's became known.

The Deportations

Birobidjan, Kirgizia and elsewhere. The trip to Kazakhstan took 3–4 weeks. Forty-six per cent are estimated to have perished in the first eighteen months. From a village of thirty families, only five had any survivors at all. Many accounts are of the families of Soviet Army soldiers being taken. In one family, a war widow with eight children, all but one girl died of hunger.

Meanwhile, back in the Crimea 'everything was done to eradicate all traces of the national life of the Tatars and even the memory of their existence. Their houses were demolished and their vines and orchards allowed to become wild and overgrown. The Tatars' cemeteries were ploughed up and their ancestors' remains torn out of the ground. . . . Everything written and printed in the Crimean Tatar language was burned, from ancient manuscripts to the classics of Marxism-Leninism. The history of the Crimea was falsified by hacks with diplomas', as an appeal by the Moscow group of intellectuals called 'Russian Friends of the Crimean Tatars' has lately put it.

The Volga-German Republic was occupied by NKVD troops in August 1941. Property was confiscated, and the inhabitants, in some areas at least, then given two hours' notice to move. In theory an allowance of a ton of luggage per family was permitted, much greater than was later to be the rule with the Asian peoples. There were a number of shootings, mainly as the result of the work of agents-provocateurs pretending to be German agents. But with the move itself the formalities were observed of stating that a simple transfer was envisaged, and that all property confiscated would be replaced in the reception areas.

The trains took a very long time. One German deportee from Mariupol speaks of a fortnight between that city and Penza, merely. On arrival in Kazakhstan and elsewhere reports are unanimous that the Germans were well treated by the local population, in spite of its own poverty. But it was a frightful ordeal, even so.

The Germans of the Crimea began to be evacuated on 20 August 1941, first to the North Caucasus and in October to Kazakhstan. On 20 October 1941 the Germans of the Caucasus followed. On 16 March 1944 it became possible to deport the

Soviet Germans who had been in Leningrad during the siege; they went to Siberia. Only the Germans between the Dnieper and the Dniester remained. They were evacuated to Germany during the German retreat and about a quarter of a million were brought back to the Soviet Union after the war and mostly sent to camps in Siberia and the Komi area. They are said to have suffered particularly in the famine of 1947.

Wolfgang Leonhard describes a brief visit in 1941 to one of the deportation areas for Germans.[12] He himself was a Communist and, though most even of the German Communists in Moscow were being compulsorily resettled, he was himself technically exempt, being required as a propagandist by the Russians. But he was induced to travel with the deportees and describes how after twenty-two days in a cattle-truck with some fifty others they arrived near Ossokarovka, about seventy-five miles north of Karaganda. Before he managed to extricate himself he was marched with the others about fifteen miles to 'Settlement no. 5'. This was an area to which, in the early thirties, deported kulaks had been sent. When these had arrived, they told Leonhard, there was nothing but bare ground. They had dug holes in the earth to live in. Many had died of cold and hunger, but now they had constructed clay huts and the survivors were scraping a living. The Germans had been billeted on these outcasts. The huts were of mud, without windows and with a single opening which was simply stopped up in winter. When Leonhard had managed to get to Karaganda he met various other Germans who had been in these places. Many of them were getting far less than their minimal official ration and had been allotted huts and outhouses which even the kulak deportees no longer found habitable. The cold was, at this time, becoming intense.

Volga Germans are also reported over a very wide area. They were, of course, in very large numbers, especially if we include Germans deported from other areas who might well be mentioned under the same general term. It seems not unlikely that returning prisoners-of-war especially may have been more alert to the presence of their co-linguists. In any case, many more reports of their presence have been published – from Kostroma, Kemerovo, Yakutsk, Krasnoyarsk, Chelyabinsk, Novosibirsk, Karaganda, Balkhash, Temir Tau, Kustanai and elsewhere. Here again practically all the possible territories seem to have received scattered groups. It is incidentally reported that the Volga Germans were not subject to military call-up until 1954, when they were once again taken into the forces for menial tasks.

This early deportation of the Germans was more a precaution than a punishment.* And their treatment was throughout better than that of later deportees. In many cases these were not billeted anywhere. They were simply marched to empty stretches of country, given agricultural implements and told to produce. In fact, they were subjected to the same measures as the original kulak deportees, and the survivors built themselves the same holes in the ground and mud huts.

This applied even to the Greeks, who were deported long after the war, when it might have been thought possible to make better arrangements. But, if it comes to that, there were complaints from the 'volunteer' settlers on the Virgin Lands, who are supposed to be under special Government auspices as an élite of Young Communists, that everything was lacking in their new settlements. If even favoured groups are so neglected, it is not to be expected that much trouble should be taken about the deportee pariahs.

Unlike the other nations, the Meskhetians, it will be remembered, were not under any accusation. And on arrival in Uzbekistan, Kazakhstan and elsewhere they were not at first subjected to NKVD 'Special Settlement' control, though conditions, especially in their main deportation area, the Uzbek 'Hungry Steppe', were bad. But this control was introduced after about six months, and largely from that time they began to suffer heavily, losing about 50,000 dead.[14] No knowledge of this whole operation then reached the West, though by about 1950 there were rumours that at some unspecified date Turks had been deported from the Caucasian area.

* An extraordinary circumstance is that Volga-German Communists, or some of them, seem to have kept their party membership, being censured and excluded from executive position, but required to continue under Party discipline.[13]

The deportation of the Greeks, which took place in 1949, has never been mentioned officially in the USSR. The article on Greeks in the second edition of the *Large Soviet Encyclopaedia*[15] mentions the existence of Greeks in the Soviet Union in the form that there are Greeks outside Greece and Cyprus 'in Turkey (in Istanbul), in Egypt (particularly Alexandria), in the USSR and elsewhere'. It may be of some significance that, unlike the case with Turkey and Egypt, no reference is made to the *location* of the Soviet Greeks. In fact before deportation they lived almost entirely on the coasts of the Black Sea and the Sea of Azov – Mariupol, now called Zhdanov, being at one time an almost wholly Greek city. The equivalent article in the first edition of the *Encyclopaedia*, Volume 19, mentions them in Mariupol (64,238 of them), other regions of the Ukraine (72,032) and the Caucasus (52,654) with others scattered elsewhere.

There is one small piece of published information which may refer to the deportation of the Greeks. *Izvestia* of 4 October 1949 lists a series of awards made to officers of the MVD and MGB for carrying out 'a special Government mission': two lieutenant-generals and three major-generals are named. Few security operations had been carried out recently on a scale involving such a number of high officers. The 'Leningrad Affair', which is said to have resulted in the shooting of up to 3,000 members of the Communist Party in that city, was then still under way, and on the face of it would anyhow seem to have been an MGB operation pure and simple. It is true that operations against partisans, and mass deportations, were then taking place in the Baltic States as well. But it is at least possible that the Greek operation is referred to.

The award of high orders to the police generals in charge of deportations is certainly traditional. Serov, who immediately after the Chechen-Ingush operation received the Order of Suvorov, officially reserved for major victories in the field, was in charge of all the deportations and then of anti-partisan activity in Lithuania. His chief subordinates, Goglidze and Gvishiani, were also decorated, as was Kobulov, who is believed to have assisted in the Crimean deportation.

The deportation of the Greeks was the last of the major operations. The Greek population of the USSR was 285,000 in 1940. The Greeks in the Crimea, about 10,000 in number, had already been sent to Kazakhstan in 1944.

Many from other areas had been sent east earlier, and others had left the country. There remained about 40,000 Greeks in the Caucasus – mainly in the towns of the Black Sea coast of Georgia. These were rounded up at two hours' notice on 14 June 1949. They were sent mainly to Kazakhstan.

More was heard from them than from most of the deportees, owing to their links with their homeland. (About 17,000 of them were actually Greek citizens.) They were able to smuggle a few letters to relations. Two of these may be quoted as descriptions which must stand for the fate of the many other races who had preceded them to Kazakhstan. One tells of the deportation itself:

> We travelled seventeen days, exposed to cold, hunger and thirst. Many of our fellow deportees died in the trains . . . . We have been brought into the desert. There are no built-up houses. The water is not drinkable and many children have already died.

The following from another letter gives some idea of the conditions of exile:

> At the Kolkhoz where we are forced to work the norms are very high. For a 'day's wage' we have to do the equivalent of three or four days' work. For one 'day's wage' they give us a kilo of corn and nothing more . . . . There is no firewood in this desert. What shall we do during the winter?

8

COMMUNISM AND
THE NATIONAL QUESTION

As the small peoples of the Caucasus and the Crimea thus went for years and decades into the oblivion of a miserable exile, some of those who learned of the deportations may have wondered how they could be reconciled with the 'Socialist humanism' often mentioned in the Soviet press, or even with Marxist principles.

And yet the Soviet regime has never undertaken measures, however ruthless, of which it cannot be argued that they are in accord with its theoretical principles. Its treatment of the Chechens and other nations has political and ideological roots which go deep into the whole Marxist-Leninist outlook. What is basic is that the Communists' attitude to national sentiment is centred on the fact that they regard it as subsidiary and temporary. In its article on 'Nation' the *Large Soviet Encyclopaedia* (2nd edition, Vol. 29 (November 1954), p. 307) says:

> Nations first arose in the period of the liquidation of feudalism and the development of capitalism. People consolidated themselves into nations not in accordance with their own desires, by the will of governments or the activity of any other subjective factors, but only as the result of the action of the objective laws of economic development.

This is merely restating Stalin's dictum: 'A nation is not merely a historical category, but a historical category belonging to a definite epoch, the epoch of rising capitalism.'[1]

Lenin made the same point, though in an even more crudely 'economic' way, when he said:

> Throughout the world, the period of the final victory of capitalism over feudalism was linked up with national move-

ments. The economic basis of these movements is that in order to achieve complete victory for commodity production the bourgeoisie must capture the home market, must have politically united territories with a population speaking the same language, while all obstacles to the development of this language and to its consolidation in literature are removed.[2]

Thus the Communists regard the nation as a phenomenon arising at a certain stage of historical development. Nations, and their wish for independent sovereign States, did not exist before bourgeois class-consciousness; and in post-bourgeois times, when the Communists are in control, national consciousness will become obsolete. As Lenin says:

The aim of Socialism is not only to abolish the present division of mankind into small States, and all-national isolation, not only to bring the nations closer to each other, but also to merge them.[3]

He elsewhere maintains that capitalism has two effects on the development of nations. It not merely produces them, but also accelerates the breakdown of national barriers so that it destroys national seclusion and substitutes class antagonism for national antagonism. 'It is therefore perfectly true that in the developed countries the working men have no country.'[4] The national question is thus seen as an inessential survival and as part of the epoch of 'bourgeois democratic' revolution rather than one which concerns the final state of the proletarian revolution. On the issue in Russian circumstances Lenin says:

In eastern Europe and in Asia the period of bourgeois-democratic revolutions started only in 1905. The revolutions in Russia, Persia and China, the wars in the Balkans, such is the chain of world events of *our* period in our 'Orient'. And only the blind can fail to see the awakening of a *whole series* of bourgeois-democratic national movements, striving to create nationally independent and nationally united States in this chain of events. It is precisely and solely because Russia and the neighbouring countries are passing through this epoch that we require an item in our programme on the right of nations to self-determination.[5]

Support for national movements of the type now described by Lenin as arising in the peripheral nationalities of Russia, like the Chechens and Crimeans, is thus regarded by Communists as tactically necessary only in an intermediate stage. Where this stage can be avoided, as in dependent countries with no active bourgeoisie, the question need never arise. An example given by Lenin from Marx is:

> If capitalism in England had been overthrown as quickly as Marx first expected, there would have been no place for a bourgeois-democratic and general national movement in Ireland. But since it arose, Marx advises the British workers to support it.[6]

Having admitted that national aspirations do exist over an undefined transitional period, Lenin immediately considers how to utilize them. It was, indeed, in connection with nationalist movements that he said:

> The General Staffs in the present war assiduously strive to utilize all national and revolutionary movements in the camp of their enemy: the Germans utilize the Irish Rebellion, the French – the Czech movement, etc. From their standpoint they are acting quite properly. A serious war would not be treated seriously if advantage were not taken of the slightest weakness of the enemy, if every opportunity that presented itself were not seized, the more so since it is impossible to know beforehand at what moment, where and with what force a powder magazine will 'explode'. We would be very poor revolutionaries if, in the great proletarian war for emancipation and Socialism, we did not know how to utilize *every* popular movement against *each separate* disaster caused by imperialism in order to sharpen and extend the crisis.[7]

The crux of the matter is thus established — national movements and questions of national sovereignty are transitional phenomena of a bourgeois nature, but ones which can be utilized by the Communists in their conduct of the more important class struggle. From this the perfectly natural conclusion was drawn that it might or might not be possible to turn particular national movements to the advantage of the Communists. And those which could not be so used were to be ruthlessly opposed. Even before the Russian revolution Lenin said:

> If . . . a number of peoples were to start a Socialist revolution . . . and if *other* peoples were found to be serving as the main bulwarks of bourgeois reaction – then we would be in favour of a revolutionary war against the latter, in favour of 'crushing' them, destroying all their outposts, no matter what small national movements arose . . . .

on the grounds that

> The various demands of democracy, including self-determination, are not an absolute, they are a particle of the general democratic (at present general Socialist) world movement. In individual concrete cases, a particle may contradict the whole; if it does, then it must be rejected.

And any particular national movement might be sacrificed, on the principle that:

> . . . the interests of the democracy of *one* country must be subordinated to the interests of the democracy of *several and of all* countries.[8]

Lenin was not, of course, doing anything very new. Marx and Engels had supported the Polish and Hungarian national movements of the previous century, but had opposed those of the Czechs and South Slavs, as Stalin points out:

> In the forties of the last century Marx supported the national movement of the Poles and Hungarians and was opposed to the national movement of the Czechs and the South Slavs. Why? Because the Czechs and the South Slavs were then 'reactionary nations'.[9]

In Marx's time it was, of course, the Germans who were thought of as the progressive nation, and Marx said that

> Except for the Poles, the Russians, and at best the Slavs in Turkey, no Slavic people has a future, for the simple reason that all Slavs lack the most basic historic, geographic, political and industrial prerequisites for independence and vitality.[10]

Engels even wrote:

> Now you may ask me whether I have no sympathy whatever for the small Slavic peoples, and remnants of peoples . . . . In fact, I have damned little sympathy for them.[11]

Lenin, too, approved this early discrimination between nations on tactical or economic grounds. For example, he points out that Marx supported the liberation movement in Poland merely as a temporary expedient until progress should take place in Russia, after which Poland would lose its importance – for the good Marxist reason that Russia was a more industrialized power. Basing himself on previous Marxist teaching he insisted that:

> As long as the masses of the people in Russia and in most Slavic countries were still fast asleep, as long as *there were no* independent, mass, democratic movements in these countries, the *aristocratic* liberation movement in Poland assumed enormous, paramount importance . . . .
>
> In general the attitude of Marx and Engels to the national question was strictly critical, and they recognized its historical relativity. Thus, Engels wrote to Marx on 23 May 1851, that . . . the significance of Poland was temporary, that it would last only until the agrarian revolution in Russia. . . . In Russia there were more elements of civilization, education, industry and of the bourgeoisie than in 'aristocratic Poland'.[12]

The view of the sacrifice of national to other considerations put forward by Lenin was developed at length by Stalin, who became the Bolshevik theorist on the national question – and remains so to this day.

Some of Stalin's works, such as the *Short Course History of the Communist Party* and *Economic Problems of Socialism*, were repudiated in Khrushchev's time. But his formulations on the national question were not criticized in any way even then, and they remain entirely authoritative. Indeed, it would be difficult for this to be otherwise, since the crucial essay in *Marxism and the National and Colonial Question* was written in pre-revolutionary times and approved by Lenin. And Lenin, of course, appointed him Commissar for Nationalities in the first Soviet Government in 1917.

Dotting the *i*'s of Lenin's theories, Stalin writes:

> This does not mean, of course, that the proletariat must support *every* national movement, everywhere and always, in every individual concrete case. It means that support must be given to such national movements as tend to weaken, to overthrow imperialism, and not to strengthen and preserve it. Cases occur when the national movements in certain oppressed countries come into conflict with the interests of the development of the proletarian movement. In such cases support is, of course, entirely out of the question. The question of the rights of nations is not an isolated, self-sufficient question; it is a part of the general problem of the proletarian revolution, subordinate to the whole, and must be considered from the point of view of the whole.[13]

And again:

> It should be borne in mind that in addition to the right of nations to self-determination, there is also the right of the working class to consolidate its power, and the right of self-determination is subordinate to this latter right. There are cases when the right of self-determination conflicts with another, a higher right – the right of the working class that has come to power to consolidate that power. In such cases – this must be said bluntly – the right of self-determination cannot and must not serve as an obstacle to the working class in exercising its right to dictatorship.[14]

This theme, so often repeated, is absolutely basic to the Communist view of the nation. How consistently it has been maintained may be seen by comparing the passages from Stalin and Lenin with an article which appeared after Stalin's death during a period of comparative 'anti-Stalinism',[15] which repeated the views of Stalin on nationality. The striking thing is that in this very long article Stalin himself is not mentioned at all while Lenin is quoted frequently. What is significant is that while thus, in effect, repudiating the dead dictator his basic thesis on the subordination of national rights to the interests of the Party was still strongly insisted on: 'The national question is subordinated to the more general and fundamental question of the socialist revolution and the Dictatorship of the Proletariat.' In addition the article made the other old points – about the progressive role of Russian influence in the history of the minorities even in Tsarist times, about the dangers of bourgeois nationalism ('tendencies . . . engendered by pressure from the exploiting classes and their agents who incite national difference and enmity among the working people of various nationalities with a view to restoring capitalism') and so on.

The general thesis that reactionary nations should not have their interests considered, which is still correct doctrine, had been put forward, as we have seen, even before there was a 'socialist' state, at a time when 'progressive' countries simply had larger proletariats or bigger socialist parties. *A fortiori*, when one state is actually in the power of the Communist Party the interests of rival nations are not to be considered where they clash with those of the Communist state – particularly as it is in the interests of the revolution for the latter to enlarge itself. Immediately after the revolution, Lenin wrote:

There is not a single Marxist who, without making a total break with the foundations of Marxism and Socialism, could deny that the interests of Socialism are above the interests of the right of nations to self-determination. Our Socialist Republic has done and is continuing to do everything possible for implementing the right of self-determination for Finland, Ukraine, etc. But if the concrete position that has arisen is such that the existence of the Socialist Republic is endangered at a given moment in respect of an infringement of the right to self-determination of a few nations (Poland, Lithuania,

Courland, etc.) then it stands to reason that the interests of the preservation of the Socialist Republic must take preference.[16]

Not only did all national movements opposed to Soviet centralism automatically become subject to legitimate destruction on the grounds that they hampered progress to 'Socialism', but it was definitely stated that national aspirations to sovereignty and independence in areas which the Tsars had ruled were reprehensible and meaningless. In 1920 Stalin issued the simple ultimatum:

When a life-and-death struggle is developing between proletarian Russia and the Imperialist *Entente*, there are only two possible outcomes for the border regions:

Either they go along with Russia, and then the toiling masses of the border regions will be freed from imperialist oppression;

Or they go along with the *Entente*, and then the yoke of imperialism will be inevitable.

There is no third course. The supposed independence of supposedly independent Georgia, Armenia, Poland, Finland, etc., is only an illusion, and conceals the utter dependence of these apologies for States on one or another group of imperialists.[17]

Indeed, he added the following year, even the formation of States such as Czechoslovakia and Yugoslavia, outside the old Russian sphere,

did not, and could not, bring about the peaceful co-existence of nationalities; it did not, and could not, eliminate either national inequality or national oppression, for the new national States, being based on private property and class inequality, cannot exist: (*a*) without oppressing their national minorities . . . (*b*) without enlarging their territories at the expense of their neighbours, which gives rise to conflicts and wars . . . and (*c*) without submitting to the financial, economic and military domination of the 'great' imperialist Powers.[18]

This schematic attitude to national sentiment, on the part of politicians who themselves had little use for it, resulted in an underestimate of its powers. This mis-evaluation has bedevilled Communist policy for decades; yet it is repeated again and again, as in Hungary and Czechoslovakia. An explicit anaysis, of what would satisfy national feeling was made by Stalin early in his career, and became the basis of Soviet tactics in attempting to appease the minorities. Its inadequacy is startling:

> A minority is discontented not because there is no national union but because it does not enjoy the right to use its native language. Permit it to use its native language and the discontent will pass of itself. A minority is discontented not because there is no artificial union but because it does not possess its own schools. Give it its own schools and all grounds for discontent will disappear.[19]

We shall see that Soviet forms give none of the realities of autonomy to the peoples concerned. It now appears that this was not originally due to some Machiavellian cunning, but that the Communists really believed that national aspirations would be satisfied by certain minimal concessions.

As to the actual form of the state in multinational Russia, the original view of the Bolsheviks was hostile to a federal solution. Lenin stated in 1913:

> Federation means a union of equals depending upon consent. . . . We reject federation on principle; it weakens economic links; it is an unsuitable form for our State.[20]

This is, of course, contrary to the later development of the Soviet Constitution, in which the 'Union' republics are, formally speaking, given the right to secede.

Stalin gave the following very illuminating reasons for the apparent revision of policy:

> *First*, the fact that at the time of the October Revolution a number of the nationalities of Russia were actually in a state of complete secession and complete isolation from one

another, and, in view of this, federation represented a step forward from the division of the working masses of these nationalities to their closer union, their amalgamation.

Secondly, the fact that the very forms of federation which suggested themselves in the course of Soviet development proved by no means so contradictory to the aim of closer economic unity between the working masses of the nationalities of Russia as might have appeared formerly, and even did not contradict this aim at all, as was subsequently demonstrated in practice.

Thirdly, the fact that the national movement had proved to be far more weighty a factor and the process of amalgamation of nations far more complicated than might have appeared formerly, in the period prior to the war, or in the period prior to the October Revolution.[21]

The second point, that the *forms* of federation may be combined with the actuality of centralization, is particularly significant.

The USSR was now formed from four theoretically independent States – the RSFSR, the Ukraine, Byelorussia and the Transcaucasian Federation – to which it had been hoped to join at least a Soviet Poland and Latvia, and possibly a whole string of European states. The incorporation of the latter was seen to require a solution even looser in appearance than federation. Stalin wrote to Lenin in 1920:

> Let us assume the future existence of a Soviet Germany, a Soviet Poland, a Soviet Hungary or a Soviet Finland; these nations which had their own state and their own army . . . will, even as Soviet States, hardly agree to enter into an immediate federation with Soviet Russia after the manner of the Bashkirs or Ukrainians.[22]

What had happened in several years of revolutionary experience was that the Bolsheviks had discovered that national feeling was too strong to make bare-faced centralization feasible, but that there was a possibility of utilizing constitutional forms of extremely liberal appearance, while preserving the substance of control intact through extra-constitutional apparatus.

Stalin had already reconciled the contradiction between the Communist general emancipatory programme and the practice of forced unity as follows:

> Thus, our views on the national question can be reduced to the following propositions:
> (a) Recognition of the right of nations to secession;
> (b) Regional autonomy for nations remaining with the given State;
> (c) Special legislation guaranteeing freedom of development for national minorities;
> (d) A single, indivisible proletarian collective, a single party. . . .
> It would be impermissible to confuse the question of the *right* of nations freely to secede with the question of whether a nation must *necessarily* secede at any given moment. This latter question must be settled quite separately by the party of the proletariat in each particular case, according to the circumstances. Thus we are at liberty to agitate for or against secession in accordance with the interests of the proletariat, of the proletarian revolution.[23]

It was his point (d) which was decisive.

Even before the formation of the USSR, when the Ukraine was supposed to be an independent republic, Lenin made a well-known complaint which shows that he did not envisage much local freedom of action and relied on the Party apparatus to prevent it.

> The Ukraine is an independent republic. That is very good, but in party matters it sometimes – what is the politest way of saying it? – takes a roundabout course, and we have to get at them somehow, because the people there are sly, and I will not say deceive the Central Committee but somehow or other edge away from us.[24]

The method of control had already been spelt out bluntly in the Party Programme itself:

The Ukraine, Latvia, Lithuania and Byelorussia exist at the present time as separate Soviet republics. Thus is solved for now the question of state structure.

But this does not in the least mean that the Russian Communist Party should, in turn, reorganize itself as a federation of independent Communist Parties.

The Eighth Congress of the R.K.P. resolves: there must exist a *single* centralized Communist Party with a single Central Committee leading all the party work in all sections of the RSFSR. All decisions of the R.K.P. and its directing organs are unconditionally binding on all branches of the party, regardless of their national composition. The Central Committees of the Ukrainian, Latvian, Lithuanian Communists enjoy the rights of the regional committees of the party, and are entirely subordinated to the Central Committee of the R.K.P.[25]

The decision of superior bodies is binding on the parties in the local republics under the Party's present constitution also. Emissaries of the Party Presidium are often sent to carry through reorganizations in the local republics. And the Party has always had an enormous preponderance of Russians – there are more Party members in the Moscow province with its nine million inhabitants than among the whole of the twenty million population of the six Muslim republics, though, indeed, in these latter a high proportion of the membership is Russian too.

This has always been the key to Soviet centralism, and the unitary Party's leading role is now even incorporated in Article 126 of the Soviet Constitution. When the original guarantees of autonomy were made, there were local Communists who complained openly that these were meaningless in view of Party centralization.

There are certain key apparatuses, apart from the Party itself, for exercising Moscow control. One is the *Prokuratura*. The Procurator-General of the Union directly appoints the Procurator and his subordinates in all the Union Republics. Their duties are to act as public prosecutors and to check the legality of measures ordered by the authorities of the republics. They have the right to challenge all administrative enactments of these authorities.

The military organization of the USSR also ignores the republican layout and the Commanders are almost always as Russian as most of their troops – as with successive C.-in-C.s of the North Caucasus district into which Kalmykia as well as Chechniya and the other mountain nations fall.

At the time when the USSR was in the process of formation the Georgian Communist leader Makharadze stated clearly the contradiction between the centralized reality and the autonomous theory:

> There has been talk here of independent and autonomous republics. On this point it is necessary to exert the greatest caution so as to avoid any kind of exaggeration whatsoever. Comrades, it is clear to all of us, what sort of autonomy, what sort of independence this is. We have, after all, a single Party, a single central organ, which in the final resort determines absolutely everything for all the republics, even for the tiny republics, including general directives right up to the appointment of responsible leaders in this or that republic – all this derives from the one organ so that to speak under these conditions of autonomy, of independence reflects, to the highest degree, an intrinsically incomprehensible proposition.[26]

His remarks remain true to this day.

The increased liberality with paper Constitutional arrangements went with the reality of the imposition of the new regime on the border areas by Russian Communists, arms in hand. As foreseen by theory, the rights of the socialist 'big nation' were taken as paramount.

These were put concretely enough by Stalin in 1920 when he said:

> Central Russia, that hearth of world revolution, cannot hold out long without the assistance of the border regions, which abound in raw materials, fuel and foodstuffs.[27]

That Soviet power was alien to these border regions was freely conceded at the time – as again by Stalin when he wrote:

> Soviet power is not power divorced from the people; on the contrary it is the only power of its kind, having sprung from the Russian masses and being near and dear to them . . . .
>
> Soviet power must become just as near and dear to the masses of the border regions of Russia. But this requires that it should first of all be comprehensible to them.[28]

An interesting subsidiary argument with a respectable Marxist look has been developed in post-Stalin times to justify the setting up of the proletarian dictatorship in countries without a proletariat – such as, in effect, Chechniya. The proletarian dictatorship has been defined as a particular form of alliance between proletariat and peasantry, with the former in actual power. It is now said that the Russian proletariat will serve as an adequate substitute in the case of peasant nations without a proletariat of their own: 'The alliance of the Russian working class with the peasantry of all the nationalities' is the formula put forward.[29]

(Here it is worth noting that the Soviet theory of the development of primitive peoples directly into 'socialism' has been confused by the first but by no means the last of the pseudo-sciences now incorporated and ossified in orthodox Marxism, the anthropology of the American, Morgan, which Engels brought into the canon in his *Origin of the Family, Private Property and the State* – though, on the whole, this was a fairly harmless aberration, more on the lines of the ridiculous theories of Marr which for so long dominated Soviet linguistics, than actively dangerous and damaging stuff like Lysenko's biology or Zhdanov's aesthetics.)

There have been frequent Soviet admissions that border populations were actually conquered, against their will, by Russian Communist forces. For instance, the first edition of the *Encyclopaedia* says, 'During the civil war, the majority of the Buryat-Mongol masses came out against the revolution.'[30] Similarly we find it quoted that:

Detachments of Red Guards, arriving from Central Russia, helped ... to smash the bourgeois-nationalist Kokand Autonomous Government.[31]

and

Without the aid of the Russian working class and the heroic Red Army the young Soviet power in Turkmenistan and in the other national border regions unquestionably could not have overcome all its numerous enemies.[32]

Even the total absence of local Communists is conceded:

It was necessary sometimes temporarily to make use of known 'fellow-travellers' [*poputchiki*], because in the first months of the Soviet regime, in some of the more backward national districts, there were almost no local Communist cadres.[33]

And the rights and wrongs of the matter, from a Soviet viewpoint, have recently been stated with absolute clarity:

The first Bashkir Congress was called at Orenburg on 19 July 1917 .... The counter-revolutionary slogan 'Bashkiria for the Bashkirs' was raised.[34]

From this, the punitive measures taken in the Caucasus and the Crimea can be seen in perspective. The national rights of Kalmyk and Chechen do not count in the face of allegedly higher considerations.

9

CONSTITUTIONAL ARRANGEMENTS AND SOVIET PRACTICE

THE constitutional guarantees by which the deported peoples were supposed to have been distinguished from mere subject races such as those of the 'imperialist' powers had read impressively, and still do. The Soviet Union is now, on paper, a federation of equal republics representing the larger nationalities. The smaller nationalities, too, have autonomous republics and autonomous regions, which form part of the larger republics.

Article 15 of the present Soviet Constitution states: 'The sovereignty of the Union Republics is limited only in the spheres defined in Article 14 of the Constitution'. Article 14, however, reserves to the Central Government the spheres of war and peace, diplomatic relations, defence, foreign trade, State security (which, of course, overrides everything else), changes in the mutual frontiers of Republics, economic planning, credit and currency, education, and many other matters. These reserved powers are so much wider than those contained in any other federal system in the world that the Union Republics are left with no autonomy except in trivialities – and even these are frequently referred to the Central Government.

The Union Republics do not, even as legal fiction, own their own natural resources. The coal, oil, copper and agricultural land are the property of the USSR as a whole.

The influence of the smaller nations in the allegedly 'highest organ of State power', the Supreme Soviet of the USSR, is appropriately small. In the Soviet of the Union representation is on a population basis. The disadvantage to the minor nationalities of this is said to be counterbalanced by the existence of the Soviet of Nationalities, a house having supposedly equal powers with the Soviet of the Union. But here, too, there has been a tendency to discriminate against the smaller nations. Thus, whereas in the original 1923 Constitution of the USSR five representatives were allowed for each Union Republic and five for each Autonomous Republic in the Soviet of Nationalities, the proportion is now twenty-five to eleven. Nor are all of these deputies local nationals. For instance of the twenty deputies to both Chambers from Bashkiria, only eight are Bashkirs or Tatars. Moreover there are a number of points which make even these provisions worthless. Elections are not contested and only persons approved by the centralized Communist Party are eligible. (The farcical nature of these elections is well demonstrated by the fact that the Volga Germans are said to have given a 99·7 per cent vote to the Government list in 1938.) And republics are abolished and their representatives removed simply by governmental order.

Moreover the value of the representation of the minorities in the Supreme Soviet naturally depends on the powers of that body. Theoretically it is the supreme organ of government. But the fact that the Party, and in practice the Party leadership, holds the realities of rule is admitted even in the constitution. And we find that when a government decree requires to be given special authority this is provided by putting it out jointly in the name of the Council of Ministers and the Central Committee of the Party. The justification of this practice was made clear enough in a political work published by the USSR Academy of Sciences:

> In particular, specially important cases, where questions of great political importance are being settled, joint decrees of the Council of Ministers (formerly the Council of People's Commissars of the USSR) and of the Central Committee of the All-Union Communist Party (Bolsheviks) are issued. The decrees of the Government in such cases acquire the significance of Party directives. The Government act is provided then with the whole strength of the prestige enjoyed by the leading organ of the Party.[1]

This was written before Stalin's death. But in recent years Party powers have actually increased, and the signature to joint decrees has often listed the Party Central Committee before the Government, which was not the case in Stalin's time.

The Supreme Soviet is supposed to have the powers of a Western parliament. But it sits for only a few days a year. In between times it is represented by its Presidium which issues decrees later ratified by the Supreme Soviet itself. And even the Presidium is simply a ratifying body to decisions of the Party. This was shown, for example, in the expulsion of Malenkov, Molotov and the 'anti-Party group' from the Central Committee in June 1957. This was followed instantly by their dismissal from their government posts by a decree of the Presidium of the Supreme Soviet, only ratified by the Supreme Soviet proper on 20 December; and similarly with the ousting of Khruschchev. There has never been an instance of the Supreme Soviet rejecting any decree issued by this Presidium.

It can be deduced that the constitutional arrangements of the USSR are not, at present, of the slightest real significance. We should seek the realities of rule and of policy elsewhere.

After the formation of the USSR, things settled down, and such formal changes as have since taken place are of minor importance. In practice, though, a considerable evolution has come about. This we have already seen demonstrated in the case of the Chechens and others, whose national feelings were at first allowed a measure of expression and whose history was at first treated sympathetically, with the gradual change to the imposition of active subservience, even in words, to Russia proper.

The central theme of Soviet policy towards the smaller nations of the Union was expressed succinctly by Kalinin thus:

> The aim of Soviet policy has always been to teach the people of the Kirgiz steppe, the small Uzbek cotton grower, and the Turkmenian gardener to accept the ideals of the Leningrad worker.[2]

If this is taken sociologically we may consider it as merely indicating the proletarianization of national cultures – a sort of first step towards that dissolution of national peculiarities which Lenin foresaw. But during the process of the imposition of the

E

ideals of the Russian worker the fact of his being Russian began
to count as much as, and then more than, his working-class
status. For national feelings exist to be utilized, in the Communist view, and when it became apparent that local nationalism was far stronger and more persistent than the Communist
leaders had hoped, it was natural enough to counter it with the
one national feeling which favoured the large centralized
industrialized state: that of the Great Russians. In a general
way this fusion of claims for the Russian nation into 'Soviet
patriotism' produced a curious chauvinism *vis-à-vis* the outer
world – showing itself absurdly in such things as claims to have
invented everything and so on. Internally it resulted in a high-
pressure campaign to rewrite local history in order to prove that
Tsarist annexation had been a good thing, the imposition of the
Cyrillic alphabet, and the forced introduction of Russian words
into local vocabularies. Local writers produced eulogies of
Russia. Indeed the present 'national' anthems of the republics
(for instance those of Azerbaidzhan and Kazakhstan) actually
contain expressions of gratitude to the Russians.

That nationality is a phenomenon of the capitalist period
and that the interests of the large Communist state must prevail,
had as a corollary the view that anyone within the USSR who
spoke for the rights, or even for the genuine history, of a
minority people was not only a nationalist but a 'bourgeois
nationalist'. Indeed, the words are inseparable in all Soviet
remarks about nationalism. This resulted in a series of purges
which are still going on. A whole series of Communist leaders
fell in the thirties – including practically all the local prime
ministers, presidents and secretaries of the Communist Party.
(In the Ukraine three prime ministers went in a year.) One of
the few who had a public trial was Khodzhayev, Prime Minister
of Uzbekistan, who confessed, among other things, to have
'planned to develop industry . . . in such a way as to be more
economically independent . . . of the Soviet Union'. At the
same time that the political leaders fell, all the cultural institutions were purged.

If we look at the map of the Communist world we see a
number of rather curious things about it. In principle the pro-

ponents of world socialism, including Marx, have thought either in terms of a world state or of a federation in which component states are provided for every important nation. We see, on the contrary, two great empires with a frontier between them that was accidentally reached on a power basis by their imperialist predecessors. Moreover, these frontiers partition big nations. If there can be a Communist Russia and a Communist China, one might ask why there could not be a Communist Turkestan. Instead the Turki peoples of the area are divided into two – even using different alphabets. For the huge area inhabited by Mongols it is worse still. They are partitioned into three separate states: an autonomous republic in the USSR, a 'People's Republic', and an 'autonomous area' in China. The temporarily independent states of the Caucasus were forced into the Soviet Union, and the Baltic States, after a much longer period of independence, were also annexed.

In foreign policy the Soviet view of the overriding interests of the larger state were expressed in the Nazi–Soviet Pact, which spoke of the 'State interests' of the two powers over the territories of Poland and the Baltic States, then independent countries. In fact there was a curious piece of dickering whereby the German claim to Lithuania was sold to the Russians for a slice of Poland and some money compensation. At the same time there was a lot of discussion as to where the Soviet sphere of influence in Asia should be, Molotov claiming expansion southwards 'in the direction of the Persian Gulf'. (The annexation of the Baltic States was in violation of treaties 'renouncing all rights of sovereignty for ever', a non-aggression pact and convention defining aggression, and mutual assistance pacts signed in 1939.)

There is another widespread phenomenon in Soviet Asia, which is particularly germane to the areas of the deported nations, that is, the influx of Russian and Ukrainian settlers. In Kazakhstan and Kirgizia, local nationalities were well in the majority in the twenties, but were barely holding their own by the end of the thirties; and the new influx into the 'Virgin Lands' initiated by Khrushchev in 1954 has further affected the position. The elections to the Kazakh Supreme Soviet – the showpiece of local autonomy – in March 1967 produced 231 European delegates to 228 Central Asians (and 1 Korean). Russian influence in the Party, the State, the police and industry is very much greater than this.

If this goes much further it may even lead to the official down-grading of the Kazakh SSR. The Karelo-Finnish SSR was in 1956 reduced to an ASSR on the grounds that its population was now largely Russian: but the real importance of this incident is not with the formalities of the matter. It indicates that a Union Republic, let alone an autonomous one, cannot complain about being swamped by Russian immigrants and then being abolished. If we consider the case of the returning Chechens, it seems plain that the implication about not upsetting the economic interests of the Russian settlers who have taken their lands (see pp. 146–7) may well mean that no real withdrawal of the latter was contemplated at all, and the Chechens had to make do as best they could, like the Kazakhs.

A further aspect of Soviet policy in this matter is the use of the most Russianized towns available for the capitals of the various republics. Baku in Azerbaidzhan, Frunze in Kirgizia, Dushambe in Tadzhikistan, Makhachkala in Daghestan, are towns with a very high proportion of Russian inhabitants. Grozny, capital of Chechniya, and Petrozavodsk, capital of Karelia, are Russian towns with Russian names. In some cases capitals have been transferred to suit this tendency – the Uzbek capital was moved from Samarkand to semi-European Tashkent in 1930, and the Volga-German capital from Markstadt to the Slav Pokrovsk in 1922; and, to take a smaller territory, the administration of the Udmurt Autonomous Province was moved from the traditional capital of Glasov to the old Russian industrial town of Izhevsk.

That economic development of a backward area need not necessarily confer any blessings on the local population is admitted in Soviet writings; it may be carried out by a big Power for 'selfish motives', and constitute 'an encroachment on the national sovereignty of the recipient country'.[3]

This particular argument was, of course, used of Britain and France. Yet it remains to be proved that Soviet economic rule has brought particular benefits. In certain cases it clearly has not. For example, 'The present-day Khakassians living in the Khakassian Autonomous Province are a minority in the national composition of Khakassia. The non-Khakassian population of Khakassia forms a majority and outnumbers the Khakassians several times. This has occurred during the last twenty years chiefly because the Khakassians, few in number, were not in a position to ensure the rapid development of a powerful industry having All-Union and All-State importance, for the establishment of which favourable local conditions exist. This circumstance brought about a great influx of non-Khakassians, principally Russians, into Khakassia. The few Khakassians found themselves interspersed among a non-Khakassian majority. . . . The percentage of Khakassians in the population of the towns of Abakan [the capital], Chernogorsk and the workers' settlements of Khakassia is quite insignificant. . . . What has been said of the Khakassians is also applicable to the Shors of Kemerovo Province . . . and the Altais of the High Altai Autonomous Province. . . . It is difficult to say what will be the ultimate fate of each of the small ethnographic groups and peoples. . . .'[4]

It is in the linguistic and cultural field that it is sometimes claimed, even by those who realize its political insignificance, that the Soviet idea of autonomy gives results. The figures are not available for the newly repatriated nations but, among their neighbours, only the following percentages of pupils received their education in the native tongue as early as 1958, since when things seem to have got worse:

Kabardine-Balkar ASSR-	-	-	24	(in Kabardinian)
Adygei Autonomous Province -	-	11	(in Adygei)
Karachai-Cherkess Autonomous Province	-	-	-	-	9	(in Circassian)
North Ossetian ASSR	-	-	-	19	(in Ossetian)[5]

We may thus summarize the whole Soviet position on nationality as follows. Communist theory presents the national question as secondary and ephemeral. National interests are to be sacrificed where necessary to the interests of the proletarian revolution. These are normally to be identified with the interests of large Communist nations.

Nevertheless, national sentiment must be 'utilized' where possible. And in multinational Communist states constitutional arrangements should be made which give every apparent concession to local feeling that does not affect the substance of centralized control. The formula used – 'national in form, Socialist in context' – may be interpreted as 'loyalty to the large Communist nation expressed in the language of the small nation'. The constitutional arrangements, formally interpreted, might seem to contradict the theory behind the Communist attitude. But practice is, in reality, completely in accord with theory.

All the same practical policy may vary. Though the leadership remains united on the central issue of never granting the substance of autonomy, there may be divergencies about how much even of the shadow to grant. For to talk too much about a minority's freedom or its revolutionary past, may (and does) encourage thoughts of real freedom and of a revolutionary future. On the other hand to suppress all this and insist on overt obeisance to all things Russian may (and does) produce resentment of an equally nationalist character. There are also, in extreme cases of repression like the deportations, considerations of the propaganda effect in non-Communist countries.

Of the post-Stalin leadership it was Beria who became most closely identified with a policy of greater concessions to the smaller nationalities of the Soviet Union. He reinstated, in Georgia, a number of leaders who had been 'victims' of 'a provocative affair concerning a non-existent nationalism', and arrested or degraded their persecutors. When he himself fell he was charged, among other things, with

> a number of criminal measures to step up the activity of the remnant of bourgeois-nationalist elements in the Union Republics, to sow enmity and discord between the peoples of the USSR and, in the first place, to undermine the friendship of the peoples of the USSR with the Great Russian people.

A few weeks before the coup against Beria, L. G. Melnikov, First Secretary of the Ukrainian Communist Party and a candidate member of the Party Presidium of the CPSU, was dismissed from all his posts for 'distortions' and 'gross errors' of a Russifying type in 'carrying out the nationality policy of the Party'. Though Beria seems to have made the running in this case (and Meshik, his then representative in the Ukraine, was later shot with him) he could scarcely have brought down this important figure without the support or acquiescence of the other members of the Presidium. Nor, when Beria fell, was Melnikov fully reinstated. It is true that he did then get another post – as Ambassador in Rumania – but he has never been restored even to full membership of the Central Committee (although he again became a minister and later was sent as economic boss of Kazakhstan, a significant post for a notorious Russifier, especially in connection with the influx of Russians in the Virgin Lands campaign. There he was severely censured and 'punished' for economic malpractices in 1958, apparently as an example to others).

This, and other considerations, seem to show that though the Presidium majority condemned Beria's concessions to national feeling, they did not favour, either, the other extreme of naked Russian domination – Stalin's policy. And this willingness to concede more of the appearance, if not much in the way of substance, has been a fairly constant attitude of the regime through all the post-Beria years. The present attitude to Shamil, gone into in Chapter 11, is a fair indication of the position. The rehabilitation of the deported peoples was the last and most important move in the abandonment of naked aggression against the nationalities. And the position is now roughly what it was in the mid-Stalin period – after he had fully established the primacy of the Russians, but before he had laid down their right to dominate entirely. 'Bourgeois nationalism' remains the great enemy. But it is no longer to be combated by repression alone.

Taken at its most abstract there is at least something to be said for the Soviet theory. On a very long-term view it may well be possible to look on nationality and national feeling as temporary phenomena, and to envisage the rise of a world language and a world culture in which the best of present national cultures is subsumed, at least to an extent. In a few thousand years, indeed, such changes might well be expected to occur. But, just the same, to look forward to that and to attempt to force them, to regard such things as having anything whatever to do with immediate issues is a little peculiar. Such developments could only be long, spontaneous and taking place in ways which we are unable to foresee, let alone compel.

It is also true that the extremes of nationalism produce unworthy results, and that some form of loyalty to an overriding conception of mankind as a whole is praiseworthy. Yet here the Soviet theorists seem to combine the worst of both worlds. They acclaim the nationalisms which they hope to use politically against their opponents and they suppress local nationalisms of which they disapprove – and not, in practice, in favour of the world as a whole, but in favour of 'Soviet patriotism', a larger but not for that reason more reputable insularity than those of the smaller peoples. And even if largeness were a virtue it is only this one largeness which is permitted – the natural solidarities of the Turkic or Mongol peoples are disrupted rather than encouraged.

For, in the first place the Soviet attitude is cynical: it wishes to exploit or delude those who feel national sentiments. And secondly, like all such cynicisms, this has led to obtuseness: the Soviet leaders have misunderstood and underestimated the power of feelings which are outside their own experience. The result has been shallow calculations, and these have not worked. National feeling has remained unsatisfied in the USSR. After twenty years of empty phrases the Chechens showed that for them the realities had never been obscured. After thirty-five years, the nationalist students of favoured Georgia demonstrated in the streets of their capital.

At the very time when the rehabilitations were proceeding various pronouncements made it clear that nationalism was recognized to be, still, a major and undying danger. The Secretary of the Communist Party of Armenia, B. Sarkisov, warned against new and 'subtle' ideological arguments of the nationalists.[6] A report of a session of the Komsomol Central Committee in Estonia carried warnings in similar terms.[7] Some of the deputies from border republics in the Supreme Soviet of the USSR also referred at this time to the dangers of the new nationalist propaganda. And so it has gone on ever since.

The point was put very strongly at the 23rd Party Congress in 1967 by, for example, V. Yu. Akhundov, First Secretary of the Azerbaidzhan Communist Party, who warned of 'the especial zeal shown by the remnants of the bourgeois nationalists, who faithfully serve those who pay them the most for slandering the Soviet people, including the Azerbaidzhan people. At times this propaganda proceeds to the keynote of "sympathy", "understanding", of certain difficulties, of a readiness to "help" in overcoming them. These gentlemen sing the praises in every way of that "paradise of national peace" that the revolution allegedly destroyed.'

The comparatively relaxed period 1961–4 had seen a number of objections to centralist tendencies raised even in the local party leaderships, faint adumbrations of the more recent Czechoslovak position. These were expressed (an authoritative statement[8] complained) in three main ways – objections to:

(a) the expansion of the non-indigenous population – i.e. Russian immigration;
(b) Russians in key positions; and
(c) the 'voluntary principle' in the study of national languages.

The language issue (arising from the School Reform Law) is essentially that of making the language of instruction voluntary from the parents' point of view (as against the old system by which both Russian and the local language were taught in schools). In effect this means that ambitious parents try to get their children into Russian language schools, which are in any case of higher quality.

The struggle over these specific issues caused trouble in Azerbaidzhan where the local First Secretary Mustafeyev was purged for 'causing bewilderment in the completely clear language question'; and in Latvia where a large 'anti-Party group' in the leadership had tried to prevent the influx of

Russian settlers and to direct the economy with local needs in mind. In Kazakhstan, 'nationalist statements' were made by the local prime minister, who was removed, together with other officials. They had apparently objected to the Russian influx into northern Kazakhstan and to the transferring of certain territory to Uzbekistan on purely economic grounds. It was presumably such proposals which resulted in a rebuff from the main ideological organ in Moscow to the effect that 'the opinion of certain comrades concerning attaching certain districts to a given republic . . . only because the majority of the population is of persons belonging to the basic nationality of the given republic, also will not withstand criticism'.[9] The Kazakhs also gave trouble over the Russian influx into the Virgin Lands. It was said of critics that 'nationalist narrow-mindedness and egotism prevent these people from seeing the role of the new territory in bringing together the nations'.[10]

The present Party Programme, adopted in 1961, is a document which flatly states the assimilationist position:

> Full-scale Communist construction constitutes a new stage in the development of national relations in the USSR in which the nations will draw still closer together until complete unity is achieved.

On the influx of Russian *colons*, it maintains:

> The appearance of new industrial centres, the prospecting and development of mineral deposits, Virgin Lands development, and the growth of all modes of transport increase the mobility of the population and promote greater intercourse between the peoples of the Soviet Union. . . . The boundaries between the Union Republics are increasingly losing their significance.

On the imposition of Russian cadres, it asserts:

> The growing scale of Communist construction calls for the continuous exchange of trained personnel among nations. Manifestations of national aloofness in the education and employment of workers of different nationalities in the Soviet republics are impermissible.

And on the language issue it states:

> The Party is called on to continue promoting the free development of the languages of the peoples of the USSR and the complete freedom for every citizen of the USSR to speak and to bring up and educate his children, in any language. . . . The Russian language has, in effect, become the common medium of intercourse and co-operation between all the peoples of the USSR.

The authoritative Party organ *Partiinaya Zhizn* of December 1962 explained that Marxists must be 'against the perpetuation of the artificial preservations of national differences'; and called for 'ruthless struggles against various survivals of nationalism' such as 'tendencies to national narrow-mindedness and exclusiveness in idealizing the national past', and it denounced, and called for the ending of, national traditions and customs which run counter to the Soviet system.

On the basic principles involved, it has been common over the whole period, and is becoming commoner now, to reaffirm the applicability of an early and blunt declaration of Lenin's, glossed here in a leading Soviet theoretical journal:[11]

> Some theoreticians who consider themselves to be internationalists, limit their internationalism merely to the recognition of the equality of rights of nations. But such 'internationalism' fits in completely with bourgeois and petty bourgeois nationalism as it fails to rise to the heights of proletarian internationalism. Lenin wrote: 'Petty bourgeois nationalism declares that internationalism is a recognition of the equality of the rights of nations and nothing more, retaining national egoism untouched (without speaking about the purely verbal character of such a recognition), whereas proletarian internationalism demands first and foremost a subordination of the interests of the proletarian fight in one country to the interests of that fight on a worldwide scale, and secondly it demands the ability and the readiness of a nation which has won victory over the bourgeoisie to go to the length of the most extreme national sacrifices for the sake of the overthrow of international capital.'[12]

The extent to which this claim is pressed at a given moment depends, of course, on circumstances. But, in principle at least, a Soviet right to intervention on a world scale is implied. This is complemented by what in Stalin's day was put as the duty of all 'proletarian internationalists' everywhere to 'defend without reservation the Soviet Union';[13] this has often been reaffirmed – in 1970 in such terms as 'At this stage too a man's attitude to the USSR and to the Communist Party of the Soviet Union remains the touchstone of his fidelity to socialist internationalism.'[14]

Thus, still, in the international sphere as much as within the Soviet Union, all considerations are subordinated to the total triumph of a group of rulers claiming to represent, in a round-about fashion, the supposed interests of a world proletariat. They have learnt little and forgotten nothing.

FIVE NATIONS REAPPEAR

THE decade of silence about the deportees was broken in 1955, with the first of a number of very slight and unimportant references which yet conceded the existence of some of these peoples, and at the same time revealed officially, for the first time, some of their new locations.

The first announcement seems to have been this note in *Kazakhstanskaya Pravda* of 17 May 1955:

> Subscription is invited for the second half-year of 1955 for a republican weekly paper 'Kinghegaman Bairakh' [Banner of Labour] published in the Chechen language. The subscription rate for 6 months is 10 roubles, 40 kopeks. Subscriptions are accepted by town departments of Soyuzpechat [Press Union] and by district offices, by communications agencies and offices, and also at points for accepting subscriptions in undertakings, collective farms, State farms and machine tractor stations.

Simply as a public reference to the Chechens, this was a step forward, though the provision of the paper itself is of no special importance: for the authorities provide propaganda sheets and lectures even in the labour camps themselves.

At first even such references were few and far between. There was a report in *Sotsialisticheski Kazakhstan* of 27 November 1955 about a Chechen-Ingush art theatre, which again marks a further advance. It seems clear that in 1955-6 all the nations concerned were released from MVD control, though not yet rehabilitated. But at some point about then the decision must have been taken to rehabilitate five of them. For the announcement that they had been wronged was made in Khrushchev's

Secret Speech of February 1956 at the Twentieth Party Congress. This was, indeed, confidential; yet its contents became widely known in the USSR. That it did not produce legislative results for nearly a year is a little curious, but in any case it certainly represented a new and less repressive approach on the part of the Soviet leaders who had hitherto been content to follow Stalin's policies.

At the Congress it had also been made clear that the deportees did not, so far, have the normal political rights of other Soviet nations. Aristov, Secretary of the Central Committee, reporting for the Credentials Committee on 16 February 1956, stated that delegates to the Congress had been elected from among a list of nationalities going down to ones as small as the Udmurts, Ossetians, Komis, Yakuts and Maris. None of the purged nations was mentioned.

Khrushchev's speech, which will be looked at later, named only the Chechens, Ingushi, Balkars, Karachai and Kalmyks as suffering peoples, making no reference to the Volga Germans, Crimean Tatars or Meskhetians. And it was of the first group only that reports were now appearing – except that nothing seems to have been said of the Kalmyks.

A further indication appeared during 1956. A *Collection of Laws of the Supreme Soviet and Decrees of the Presidium of the Supreme Soviet 1938 – July 1956* came out, passed for publication on 27 August 1956. It quoted only a few decrees having a bearing on the deported nations: a decree of 7 September 1941 partitioning the Volga-German Republic between Saratov and Stalingrad Provinces, and a decree of 30 June 1945 transforming the Crimean ASSR into the Crimean Province. That is, decisions involving the republics *not* selected for rehabilitation in the Secret Speech. Otherwise there was only one relevant decree: one of 22 March 1944 on the 'creation of Grozny Province with centre at Grozny, and liquidation in this connection of the Grozny and Kizlyar Okrugs of the Stravropol Territory', naming the raions of the abolished Okrugs (and one from Stravropol), which were to enter the new unit. Thus a reorganization of the first (hitherto unknown) post-Chechen administrative arrangements was published, but not any of the decrees actually dealing with the end of the autonomy of the Chechens – or any others of those now to be rehabilitated.

Not that the attempts at reconciliation, even with those mentionable, were going as well as all that. *Sovietskaya Kirgizia* (11 February 1956), revealing the presence of Chechens in the Kalininskoye area, complained of a lack of 'cultural and educational work among the Chechen population, a considerable number of whom still retain feudal and ancestral survivals'. The paper added that there had been no lectures at all given in Chechen over the past year.

But now other deported nations had begun to reappear. They too were in localities where unofficial reports had already placed them. *Kazakhstanskaya Pravda* of 15 April 1956 announced that the Party town committee in Kokchetav (North Kazakhstan) had organized a group of lecturers to give talks on the Twentieth Congress in the Ingush language. *Sovietskaya Kirgizia* of 19 May 1956 announced that the Kirgiz State Publishing House 'has begun to publish the works of Karachai-Balkarian writers in their native languages'. An anthology included poems by leading Karachai-Balkar poets on 'Lenin; the heroic feats of the peoples of the USSR in the great patriotic war; and the struggle for peace'. All these subjects, and in particular the second one, might be thought of as ones which the peoples concerned have little reason to be lyrical about. Then Chechens and Ingushi – 'farm workers' – were reported in the Bulaevsk raion, in the extreme north of Kazakhstan.[1]

Right up to the official announcement of the rehabilitations, these references remained sporadic. For instance, Alma Ata Radio of 18 December 1956 stated that in 1957 the Kazakh State Literary Publishing House would produce works in Russian, Kazakh, Uighur, Chechen and Ingush. The same station reported a Karachai-Balkar dance ensemble in the city on 20 January 1957. But little more than these cultural hints appeared.

Khrushchev had clearly implied that the whole deportation was a crime and should be reversed. What he said on the matter in the Secret Speech was:

Comrades, let us reach for some other facts. The Soviet Union is justly considered as a model of a multinational state because we have in practice assured the equality and friendship of all nations which live in our great fatherland.

All the more monstrous are the acts whose initiator was Stalin and which are crude violations of the basic Leninist principles of the nationality policy of the Soviet State. We refer to the mass deportations from their native places of whole nations, together with all Communists and Komsomols without any exception; this deportation action was not dictated by any military considerations.

Thus, already at the end of 1943, when there occurred a permanent break-through at the fronts of the great patriotic war in favour of the Soviet Union, a decision was taken and executed concerning the deportation of all the Karachai from the lands on which they lived. In the same period, at the end of December 1943, the same lot befell the whole population of the Autonomous Kalmyk Republic. In March 1944 all the Chechen and Ingush people were deported and the Chechen-Ingush Autonomous Republic was liquidated.

In April 1944, all Balkars were deported to faraway places from the territory of the Kabardine-Balkar Autonomous Republic and the Republic itself was renamed Autonomous Kabardine Republic. The Ukrainians avoided meeting this fate only because there were too many of them and there was no place to which to deport them. Otherwise, he would have deported them also. (Laughter and animation in the hall.)

Not only a Marxist-Leninist but also no man of common sense can grasp how it is possible to make whole nations responsible for inimical activity, including women, children, old people, Communists and Komsomols, to use mass repression against them, and to expose them to misery and suffering for the hostile acts of individual persons or groups of persons.

This statement made certain points clear. It confirmed, approximately, the dates of the deportations – giving, in addition, the Balkar date, hitherto unknown. It confirmed that some hostile activity had taken place. And it exposed the rather perfunctory attempt of the earlier decrees to imply that the work was simply a humane resettlement, by its reference to 'misery and suffering' inflicted.

More important, it foreshadowed an effort to put an end to their sufferings.

REHABILITATION

At the meeting of the Supreme Soviet in February 1957 these first rehabilitations finally went through. In his speech Gorkin (who had been a signatory of the original deportation decrees) dealt with the matter in the following terms – worth quoting as the first public statement on the matter ever put before the Soviet peoples:

By a decree of 9 January 1957 the Presidium of the Supreme Soviet of the USSR recommended the Presidium of the Supreme Soviet of the RSFSR to examine the question and take decisions:

On the reorganization of the Kabardine ASSR into the Kabardine-Balkar ASSR,

On the restoration of the Chechen-Ingush ASSR in the structure of the RSFSR,

On the formation of the Kalmyk Autonomous Province in the structure of the RSFSR,

On the reorganization of the Cherkess Autonomous Province into the Karachai-Cherkess Autonomous Province.

In accordance with these decisions the Presidium of the Supreme Soviet of the RSFSR passed Decrees on the reorganization of the Kabardine ASSR into the Kabardine-Balkar ASSR, on the restoration of the Chechen-Ingush ASSR, on the formation of a Kalmyk Autonomous Province and on the reorganization of the Cherkess Autonomous Province into the Karachai-Cherkess Autonomous Province. At the same time the Presidium of the Supreme Soviet of the RSFSR, for the direction and organization of all work connected with the restoration of autonomies, pending elections of the leading Soviet organs, confirmed organizational committees of representatives of the corresponding nationalities for the Chechen-Ingush ASSR and the Kalmyk Autonomous Province.

Direction of work for the implementation of all measures connected with the reorganization of the Kabardine ASSR into the Kabardine-Balkar ASSR and the Cherkess Autonomous Province into the Karachai-Cherkess Autonomous Province has been entrusted accordingly to the Council of Ministers of the Kabardine ASSR and the Executive Committee of the Cherkess Autonomous Province, together with representatives of the Balkar and Karachai peoples.

Comrades, deputies! The practical implementation of measures for the restoration of the national autonomy of these peoples requires a certain amount of time and the carrying out of much organizational work in the preparation of the necessary production, housing and other cultural and everyday conditions in places of former residence. Great expenditure of material and monetary funds is also required.

Therefore the resettlement of citizens of the stated nationalities who have expressed the desire to return to regions of former residence must be conducted in an organized manner, in small groups, at definite periods and in order of precedence. These periods and order of precedence, and also all practical questions of labour and everyday arrangements, will be determined and solved by organs of State power of the autonomous republics and autonomous provinces being formed.

Such an order will make it possible not to permit certain complications and to avoid difficulties for the population of these nationalities in the matter of labour and living arrangements. It should also be borne in mind that unorganized resettlement can do serious harm to the economy of those collective farms, State farms and enterprises in which workers of these nationalities are employed at the present time. It is therefore necessary to guard against all attempts at unorganized resettlement.

Proceeding from these considerations and bearing in mind the need to prepare in advance conditions of a productive and everyday order it is proposed to conduct the resettlement of citizens of Balkar, Kalmyk and Karachai nationality in the territory of the restored autonomies and organize work for them during 1957 and 1958.

As concerns Chechen and Ingush peoples, as being the most numerous, it is proposed to carry out measures connected with the restoration of their national autonomy over a longer period, between 1957 and 1960.

There is no doubt that republics, territories and provinces on whose territory the Balkars, Chechens, Ingushi, Kalmyks and Karachais are living at the present time will render the necessary assistance in the organized conduct of the resettlement of those desiring to return to their former place of residence, and at the same time will create for those people who continue to live in these republics, territories and provinces every condition for their active participation in economic and cultural construction together with other peoples of these territories and provinces.

In connexion with the restoration of the Chechen-Ingush ASSR by a Decree of 11 January 1957, the Presidium of the Supreme Soviet of the USSR has ratified a resolution of the Presidium of the Supreme Soviet of the Georgian SSR and the Presidium of the Supreme Soviet of the RSFSR on the handing over of part of the territory of the Dushet and Kazbek regions from the Georgian SSR to the RSFSR and on the restoration in such manner of the borders between these union republics which existed up to 7 March 1944.

In ratifying Decrees on the restoration of the national autonomy of the peoples mentioned it will be necessary to introduce appropriate changes into Article 22 of the Constitution of the USSR.[2]

Most of this speaks for itself. The date of 7 March 1944 refers to the then unpublished decree on the destruction and partition of the Chechen-Ingush ASSR, referred to overtly in the 1958 edition of *Territorial Administrative Divisions of the Union Republics* (see pp. 78–9), which may be the rather legalistic reason why Khrushchev gives March, instead of the well-authenticated February, as the date of the Chechen-Ingush

deportation. The retrocession of Georgian territory affected
only the area annexed from the Chechen-Ingush republic. As
far as the territories annexed by Georgia in the Karachai area
are concerned, one of the post-rehabilitation volumes of the
Encyclopaedia, Volume 47, has a short article on the Cherkess
Autonomous Province, in which it is said that

> the Karachai-Cherkess Autonomous Province was formed on
> 9 January 1957 and into it entered the former Cherkess
> Autonomous Province, the Zelenchuk, Ust-Dzhegntinski and
> Klukhori Raions of the Stravropol Territory, the rural area
> of the city of Kislovodsk and the eastern part of the Psebay
> Raion of the Krasnodar Territory.

Thus even prior to the rehabilitation laws, all Karachai lands
formed part of the Stravropol Territory of the RSFSR. Those
which had earlier gone to Georgia had been retroceded to the
RSFSR by a decree of 14 March 1955.[3] This transfer, of an
area which at the time had no expectation of Karachai return,
seems to confirm our earlier consideration of the administrative
difficulties of the previous arrangement, which had no com-
pensating advantages except in pleasing the Georgians, no
longer an important consideration after the deaths of Stalin
and Beria.

The law Georgadze proposed was passed in the following
form:

> Law on confirming the decree of the Presidium of the
> Supreme Soviet of the USSR on the restoration of the
> national autonomy of the Balkar, Chechen, Ingush, Kalmyk
> and Karachai peoples.
>
> The Supreme Soviet of the Union of Soviet Socialist
> Republics decides:
>
> Article 1. To confirm the decrees of the Presidium of the
>   Supreme Soviet of the USSR of 9 January 1957:
>   On the transformation of the Kabardine
>   ASSR into the Kabardine-Balkar ASSR.
>   On the restoration of the Chechen-Ingush
>   ASSR in the framework of the RSFSR.

On the formation of a Kalmyk Autonomous Province in the framework of the RSFSR.

On the transformation of the Cherkess Autonomous Province into the Karachai-Cherkess Autonomous Province.

Article 2. To confirm the decree of the Presidium of the Supreme Soviet of the USSR of 11 January 1957:

On the transfer of parts of the territories of the Dushet and Kazbek raions from the Georgian SSR to the framework of the RSFSR.

President of the Presidium of the Supreme Soviet of the USSR, K. Voroshilov

Secretary of the Presidium of the Supreme Soviet of the USSR, A. Gorkin

Moscow, Kremlin, 11 February 1957.[4]

A further decree of the Supreme Soviet, of 11 February 1957, runs in part as follows:

Article 2. To delete from Article 22 of the USSR Constitution the list of the administrative provinces and territories.

In this connection, and also in connection with the Law 'On the Confirmation of the Decrees of the USSR Supreme Soviet Presidium on the Restoration of the National Autonomy of the Balkar, Chechen, Ingush,' Kalmyk and Karachai Peoples', Article 22 to be read as follows:

Article 22. The RSFSR includes the Bashkir, Buryat-Mongolian, Daghestan, Kabarda-Balkar, Karelian, Komi, Mari, Mordovian, North Ossetian, Tatar, Udmurt, Chechen-Ingush, Chuvash and Yakut ASSRs and the Adygei, Gorno-Altai, Jewish, Kalmyk, Karachai-Cherkess, Tuva and Khakass Autonomous Provinces.

This completed the promised legislative processes for the moment.

The reduction of the Kalmyks to an autonomous province,

and the reversion of the Karachai from having an autonomous province of their own to sharing one again with their Cherkess neighbours certainly seemed to imply a reduction in their numbers. The precise implications were not entirely clear.

On the one hand propaganda considerations in connection with Soviet influence in Asia would ordinarily have been expected to produce the maximum effort to keep up the appearance of complete restitution. Unless the populations were very far indeed below the normal minimum one would expect administrative rules or customs to be applied with considerable latitude. In the case of the Kalmyks, for instance, it is known that Asian Governments intervening in favour of fellow Buddhists made several inquiries about their fate. One report says, indeed, that the Soviet authorities stated frankly at some stage that they could not then find more than a few hundred Kalmyks. However that may be, it may be worth looking for something in the way of an upper limit by seeing what populations were usually associated with autonomous provinces and autonomous republics respectively.

I cannot find that it has ever been laid down that a certain population goes with a certain status. On the other hand Kalinin (then President of the USSR) promised the Jews that the autonomous province of Birobidzhan which had been allotted to them would be transformed into an autonomous republic when its Jewish population reached the hundred thousand mark.[5] This seems to imply that the status depends on the number of the titular nationality in the area, and not the total population. Before the war the number of Kalmyks in the Republic had been 134,271.

But as we shall see, yet another change was to be made in the Kalmyks' status.

Meanwhile a repudiation of the other official attack on the restored nations followed. An article on 'The Party and Questions of the Development of Soviet Literature and Art' appeared in *Kommunist* of February 1957. This article, which is a strong justification in principle of the 'Zhdanovist' cultural resolutions of the Central Committee in 1946–8, makes a few reservations. One of these is 'in the resolution on the opera *The*

Great Friendship there is a wrong characterization of the Ingush and the Chechens'.

The publication of the rehabilitation decrees in February 1957 was followed by other announcements. For instance there were decrees about reorganization and renaming in the territories concerned.

A decree of 12 January 1957 on changes of name in the Kalmyk Autonomous Province of the Stavropol Territory followed.[6] The capital, Stepnoi, is changed back to its former Kalmyk name, Elista. Five other villages have changes of name but not obviously significant of de-Russification. (Indeed, one of them actually becomes Komsomolskiy.) The same issue also publishes a decree of 15 January 1957 on the administrative divisions of the Karachai-Cherkess Autonomous Province of the Stavropol Territory. Among other things the town of Klukhori becomes Karachaevsk.

Administrative Territorial Divisions of the Union Republics (Moscow, 1958) gives some interesting information about the revived republics and provinces. Like the 1941 edition, and unlike those which appeared meanwhile, it gives the populations, though not the proportions of Russian and native inhabitants. These we will consider later.

The Chechen-Ingush ASSR is given as having an area in 1958 of 19·3 thousand square kilometres as against 15·7 in 1941. The map, though on a small scale, confirms that the republic has gained much territory north of the Terek and lost some in the mountain valleys. It is now formed of seventeen rural districts instead of the twenty-three of its previous organization. Internal reorganization may have taken place (and some centres, such as Sovietskoye, have kept their Russian names) while it appears that three of the new districts are north of the Terek. (The regions of the town of Grozny, incidentally, retain their old names except that the Molotov region has now rather inappropriately been renamed Stalin.) The handbook states that the republic was abolished on 7 March 1944. This is the first time that a date had been definitely given to this decision, and presumably refers to the decree of the Presidium of the Supreme Soviet whose constitutional confirmation by the

Supreme Soviet itself was announced in *Izvestia* more than two years later. It will be noticed that even this Presidium decree was *ex post facto*, the deportations having actually taken place the previous month.

Of the restored republics the Chechen-Ingush was the only one listed whose dissolution had been previously announced – since the Crimean and Volga-German ASSRs have not been restored. And it is only in connection with the Chechen-Ingush ASSR that the volume finds it necessary to mention the facts of the dissolution, treating the other revived areas as if they had existed all the time, simply with changes of status. (Why this misleading impression should be given is not really clear even so, for the decree restoring the areas made the whole position public in any case.)

The Kalmyk Autonomous Province was given as being very little different in size from the old ASSR (75·9 thousand square kilometres as against 74·2 in 1941). On 29 July 1958 a new decree raising its status once more to that of Autonomous Soviet Socialist Republic was published in the following terms:

> To meet the wishes of the toilers of the Kalmyk Autonomous Province, and being guided by the principles of a free development of nationalities, and in accordance with part (*e*) of Article 14 of the Constitution of the USSR, the Presidium of the Supreme Soviet of the USSR decrees:
>
> 1. To confirm the changing of the Kalmyk Autonomous Province into the Kalmyk Autonomous Soviet Socialist Republic, enacted by decree of the Presidium of the Supreme Soviet of the RSFSR on 26 July 1958.
>
> 2. To submit this decree for confirmation by the Supreme Soviet of the USSR.
>
> (Signed)   President: Voroshilov
>
> Secretary: Georgadze
>
> Moscow, Kremlin, 29 July 1958.

The decisions, first to reduce the Kalmyk territory to an Autonomous Province and then to raise it again to an ASSR, contrast significantly. The natural conclusion from the original rehabilitation decree of January 1957 is that after careful consideration in the year following the statement on the matter in Khrushchev's Secret Speech, it was decided on administrative grounds that the Kalmyks no longer rated a republic. The reason can scarcely have been other than an inadequate population. It hardly seems probable that any new objective factors produced the reconsideration. In Kalmykia there were only the barest references to a few hundred here, a few thousand there. For instance, Elista Radio (29 July 1957) spoke of the return of 290 families. Even more significantly, Elista Radio on 12 June 1958, said: '*altogether* 6,000 Kalmyk families are expected to return to the province this year'. (The 1959 census figures give 106,066 Kalmyks in all, but only 64,882 of them in their ASSR.)

If administrative and demographic circumstances have not changed, the motives for the new alteration are presumably to be found on the political and propaganda side. Of all the deported nations, the spokesmen of the Kalmyks in the free world have been most numerous and most effective. They roused the interest of the governments and periodicals of much of Asia, and lobbied effectively at the Cairo and Bandung Conferences. They drew and publicized the obvious conclusion about the demotion to autonomous province, and the Soviet leaders may have felt that they had underestimated this point. Though the practical advantage to the Kalmyks of this particular change is clearly nil, it does perhaps show once more that the Soviet authorities are to some extent influenced by foreign public opinion.

However that may be, the Kalmyks were soon, as if nothing had happened, required to produce the old line in literature. *Literaturnaya Gazeta* of 29 December 1958 carried an article by N. Narmaev on the revival of Kalmyk-Soviet poetry in which he quoted some Kalmyk poetry of the Stalin period as a model:

> Hearing Lenin's words,
> The Kalmyks took up arms
> Strong and firm in fight
> They won their happiness.

Gorkin implied in his speech that the return of the smaller of the nations in question was an easier matter than the repatriation of the Chechens. And in fact the smallest – the Balkars, or some of them – began to arrive back almost immediately after the law was published. *Sovietskaya Rossiya* of 12 May 1957 reported a Balkar kolkhoz on the Cherek celebrating the return; and it announced, 'starting from April', the publication of a local newspaper *Kommunzinge Zhol* in Balkar. Smirnov's *History of Kabarda*, passed for printing in May 1957, also asserted that:

> The task of the economic rehabilitation of a significant number of Balkars was successfully carried out. The working people of the Republic showed all-sided help to the Balkars, and helped them to re-establish their kolkhozes and sovkhozes, public and private enterprises, and cultural and educational institutions. This brotherly help demonstrated the unbreakable comradeship of the peoples of the country.

Early in 1958 the British mountaineering expedition in the Caucasus actually met a Balkar who praised the regime's efforts.

The Karachai return does not seem to have been so quick. Cherkess Radio (8 April 1958) is reported as saying that preparatory work had begun for the mass return of the Karachai. Stavropol Radio has been quoted as announcing the arrival of 5,000 Karachai families late in 1957.[7]

The reorganization of education had already been dealt with by the Ministry of Education of the RSFSR, which ruled that within four years Kalmyk, Karachai, Chechen and Ingush children should be taught in their native languages in Classes I–IV, and thereafter (V–X) in Russian, but that for the moment only the first class could be taught in the native language.[8] This seems to confirm further that practically no native teachers were immediately available, and hence that normal education had not been practised in exile.

The same article, in fact, called for the organizing of classes for the 'training or retraining of primary teachers', with the obvious implication that the deportees had been complete pariahs culturally as well as politically during their years in the wilderness. This is further confirmed by an article which gave a list of scientific workers, in 1955, of all the main nationalities of the Soviet Union, including 70 Kabardines, 106 Yakuts, 90 Udmurts, 343 Ossetians, 231 Daghestan nationals, etc.[9] None of the purged nations is included. That the omission is not due to a mere desire not to mention these peoples is shown by the fact that the article goes on later to praise the Central Committee for re-establishing 'the national autonomy of the Balkar, Chechen, Ingush, Kalmyk and Karachai peoples', thus removing 'the infringements in the application of the Leninist principles of national policy which were committed during the war'.

We have already seen the meagre reports of the Kalmyk trickle home. But when it comes to the Chechens, it seems that the authorities were right to expect trouble of a different kind. At first reports gave no indication of anything but smooth progress. On 21 June 1957 Moscow Radio announced that one Chechen and one Ingush paper were appearing in Grozny. Grozny Radio of 29 October 1957 stated that 142,000 Chechens and Ingushi had 'so far settled in the autonomous republic'.

By the beginning of 1958 no regular government yet existed in the Chechen-Ingush Republic, which was ruled by an Organizing Committee. A crisis had meanwhile arisen. Instead of the 100,000 repatriates scheduled to have come back by then, some 200,000 had returned and the committee was overwhelmed.[10] Homes and work for the repatriates and schools for their children were not available. Moreover, an article published in January 1958[11] revealed other problems. 'Reactionary elements', especially supporters of old custom and of the Shariya, were preserving tribal and religious survivals and discouraging the Chechens from playing an active part in social, political and labour life. There had been a revival of polygamy – one man being mentioned as having five wives. (This may, as Kolarz has suggested, reflect the extent of the number of Chechen males to have perished – just as in Paraguay, after the wars of the dictator Lopez almost exterminated the male population, polygamy had to be introduced.)

The article also speaks of national discord, and of Chechens and Ingushi who refused to let their children join Soviet Youth Clubs and other institutions for Communist indoctrination. It attacks the resettlers, too, for their opposition to work on the collective and state farms. 'Some backward elements put their private property first and show a criminal disregard for the social property of collective and state farms.' All Communists in the area were called upon to wage a ruthless struggle against survivals from the past in the minds of the Chechens and Ingushi. But the paper admitted that even the officials chosen from the repatriates often supported 'reactionary attitudes'. In addition 'backward elements' were trying 'to re-establish private property and plundering the property of the Kolkhozes and Sovkhozes'. This at least sounds as if Chechens and Ingushi were attempting to retrieve their own possessions, and that this was not well regarded by the authorities. The whole picture was one of peoples whose alienation from the Soviet system had been strengthened rather than weakened by their sufferings.

In March 1958, the local press referred to a plenary session of the Organizing Council, which had been concerned with improving political work among the Chechens and Ingushi. 'Political agitation is very poor among women and youth on collective farms and in rural areas in general.' Anti-religious propaganda was not operating properly, and 'too little attention was being given to the spirit of the Leninist nationalities policy'.[12] A republican government was formed about this time, with Gairbekov as Chairman of the Council of Ministers (a title he is given on Moscow Radio of 16 April 1958).

A 'meeting recently held of the provincial party *Aktiv* of the Chechen-Ingush Republic' was reported in September.[13] N. G. Ignatov, member of the Presidium of the Central Committee, and of the Party Secretariat, took part – an extraordinarily high official to be present on such an occasion. 'Sharp criticism' was made of the Provincial Committee and the Grozny town committee, which had committed 'serious shortcomings' in industry, agriculture and ideological work, and the 'isolation of many Party and Soviet organs from the masses' was deplored. 'Sharp criticism' was also levelled against the provincial secretaries and against Gairbekov.

In all these reports the impression is given that the guarantee not to harm established economic interests was interpreted to mean that the Chechens, in the main, were having to fit in as best they can into Russian kolkhozes, and to provide a reserve of labour for the industries of Grozny. Right from the start, for instance, there were accounts of the building of new houses for them: Grozny Radio of 29 October 1957 spoke of 9,000 new ones with 11,500 under construction; while a few weeks later the local press mentioned 15,000 built in rural areas also, and 'thousands' under construction.[14] There is no need to assume that this is an overestimate – the houses of the area are simple, hut-like constructions. But it does seem to imply that the Chechens and Ingushi were not getting their own homes and villages back, but were rather being directed where the State desired – including the hitherto non-Chechen desert area to the north of the Terek which for the first time forms part of the republic and is shown as Chechen on ethnographical maps.

The Chechens and Ingushi, in any case, remained insufficiently grateful and docile. In August 1962 came an attack on 'the practice of the selection and deployment of cadres in Checheno-Ingushetia whereby some people, making references to "local conditions", continue to push forward, advance and watch over the interests of their "kinsmen" '. For example Gaib Mezhidov, First Secretary of the Nozhai-Yurt, and later of the Kurchaloi, District Party Committees, had put his own 'friends, countrymen and relatives' into scores of posts; a friend with two convictions had been recommended as head of the local militia; and the grandson of a sheikh and nephew of a mullah had actually been put up for the post of a departmental head of a district Party committee. A Minister in the ASSR's government had similarly lapsed. And when such men were exposed the Republican Committee first expressed shock and horror – and then promoted them.[15]

A few months later the attack was resumed. 'Responsible officials' of the local Party Committee and Government, and of the local administration, were accused of abetting such practices. A number were censured or expelled, including two Ministers, two local Party secretaries, a mayor, the head of the

consumer co-operatives, and the chairman of the local transport Trade Union.[16]

In general, the use of their positions by the newly re-estab-
lished Chechen and Ingush officials to give posts to locals was
supplemented by the perversion of such economic organs as the
meat combine to profitable private trade. Such reports remain
endemic. It is even the case that, in 1966,

> It was said at the Chechen-Ingush Oblast Party Con-
> ference that the mysterious shortcoming in the struggle against
> survivals and prejudices of the past is passivity on the part of
> the party and Soviet aktiv, connivance, softness and even
> personal participation by certain leading comrades in
> religious rites. In some places in raions of Checheno-
> Ingushetia there are still cases of polygamy, forcing women
> into marriage, kidnapping of girls, encouragement of bride-
> money, and other feudal survivals. We must create circum-
> stances of intolerance toward these shameful phenomena....[17]

It emerges clearly enough that the Chechens were un-
co-operative, addicted to ideological, social and economic
practices disliked by the regime, and in general still possessed
by a desire not to be under their present rulers.*

Soviet maps now show the Kalmyk Republic as almost
exactly on its old area. Some of the Russified names have been
changed back into Kalmyk – in particular Elista, the capital.
Others remain in their Russified form. The Karachai area,
now united with the Cherkess Autonomous Province, also
seems to occupy almost exactly its old territory. The Kabardine-
Balkar Republic is shown. It has regained from Georgia the
Balkar strip round Mount Elbrus.

A more interesting state of affairs is shown in the frontiers
farther east. Some Ingush territory taken by Ossetia has not
been regained. Instead the Chechen-Ingush ASSR has been
compensated by the much larger stretch to the north of the
Terek, where large areas are shown on the accompanying map
as 'sand'. (The whole of the sparsely inhabited desert and semi-

* Two attempts by Chechens to blow up the statue of General Yermolov
in Grozny are reported in 1969 (*Khronika*, No. 8).

desert stretch between the Terek and the Kuma formed part
of Daghestan up till the beginning of the war when it was
annexed to Russia proper. It has now been restored to Daghestan, except for the part given to the Chechen-Ingushi.)

Some light on the resettlement of the mountaineers in the
plains was thrown by an article by A. Agayev in *Literature and
Life* of May 1959. It speaks of 'the problem of resettling the hill-
man in the plains, a problem which is so burning for Daghestan

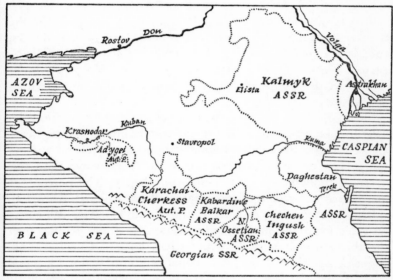

Autonomous Republics and Provinces in the North Caucasus 1958

that the CC, CPSU dealt with it at its Plenary Meeting in
December 1958. This resettlement would guarantee to all
socially gainful employment. It promises a well-to-do life and
lighter working conditions. It makes it possible to discard the
wooden plough for the tractor and the cart for the lorry. It
means roads instead of mountain paths, and good dwellings.
At the present moment the Republic's Party organization is
carrying on a tireless effort to explain the idea to the hillmen,
persuading them to resettle in the plains which take up nearly

half of this "land of mountains". But many of the hillmen, while they understand that life in the plains is a blessing, are not hastening to resettle there. In the past the plains meant foreign incursions, hostility on the part of the local population, malaria and drought. Force of habit is also a great obstacle.'

In fact they do not want to go, and the same presumably applies to the Chechens.

How Many Returned?

The figures for the deported nationalities as given in the census of January 1959 are: Chechens, 418,756; Kalmyks, 106,066; Ingushi, 105,980; Karachai, 81,403; and Balkars, 42,408. Figures for the Crimean Tatars and Volga Germans cannot be distinguished from the general Tatar and German population.

Since 1939, the Soviet population as a whole had increased – in spite of enormous losses in the war and the labour camps – from about 170,467,000 to about 208,827,000 (i.e., by about $22\frac{1}{3}$ per cent). The deported nations are in all cases worse than this average, though to a greatly differing degree. The percentage increase or decrease is approximately: Ingush, +15; Karachai, +8; Chechen, $+2\frac{1}{2}$; Balkar, 0; and Kalmyk, $-20\frac{3}{4}$. When we consider what the percentage increases for these peoples over the thirteen-year period 1926–39 had been – Chechens, 28; Ingushi, 24; Karachai, 37; Balkars, 28; and Kalmyks, 3 – it is clear that the losses must have been enormous, particularly when we consider that the period between censuses itself included a thirteen-year period, 1946–59, in which there had been no mass terror of the types accompanying collectivization or the great purge.

Unfortunately, we have no direct estimates of casualties except in the Crimean case, and these cannot be compared to the 1959 census, in which the Crimeans are not differentiated. Nevertheless it will be convenient to consider the Crimean figures at this point as the clearest indication available to us of the nature of the deportation losses. When we consider that the Crimeans appear to have risen once more to about their pre-war numbers, we have a reasonable rough criterion to apply to the others, whose losses, except for the Meskhetians and the Volga Germans, are likely to have been of the same order.

At the trials of Crimeans which took place in 1968, one of the main charges was of 'slandering' the USSR. This was based on the figure of 46·3 per cent deaths in the deportations and the eighteen months following, put forward by the Tatars in their current documents and accepted, as we have seen, by Russian liberals like Academician Sakharov. In February 1968, the Uzbek Ministry of Public Order (MOOP/MVD) sent to the KGB, in charge of the prosecutions, and to the courts concerned, figures from the old NKVD files purporting to show that the Tatar figure was much exaggerated – though it may seem odd both that even the lower figures should be thought harmless to the Soviet reputation, and that such a charge could be brought at all when no one has yet been sent to trial for the rather graver offence of actually causing the deaths in question.

The first document, dated 8 February 1968, and signed by General of Internal Security 3rd Rank Beglov,[18] states that the Crimean deportees started to reach Uzbekistan on 29 May 1944 and had in the main arrived by 8 June 1944. Figures at the beginning of July 1944 were: 35,750 families, with a total of 151,424 members. On 1 January 1945 it was 36,568 families, with a total of 134,742 members comprising 21,619 men, 47,537 women, and 65,568 children under 16.* The document adds that from 1 January 1945 to 1 January 1946 deaths amounted to 13,183 (comprising 2,562 men, 4,525 women, and 6,096 children).

General Grigorenko, commenting on this document, notes that the 151,424 figure of July 1944 had lost 16,682 dead by January 1945 in spite of a reinforcement of 818 families, and that if we subtract the estimated numbers of the latter from the January 1945 total alive, the deaths come out 3,468 higher – i.e., 20,150 for the first six months. Adding the 13,183 for the following year, we have a total of 33,333 deaths. This figure is thus an 'official' one of around 22 per cent dead.

* It will be seen that either the KGB or the transcribers or General Grigorenko have made a slight error: either way it affects the totals by eighteen only.

F

A second document, from the Deputy Head of the First Special Department of the Uzbek MOOP to the Investigation Department of Uzbek KGB, dated 5 February 1968,[19] states that no exact figures are available of deportees, but cites a report on the economy of the NKVD 'Special Settlements', giving the deaths there from May – June 1944 to 1 January 1945 as 13,592, and saying that this is 9·1 per cent dead. That is, the figure is based on the 151,424 arrivals in Uzbekistan. The year 1945 is not covered, but if we add the 13,592 of Document II to the 1945 deaths of Document I we get 26,775 – a total of about 18 per cent – i.e., lower than the other 'official' figure, but in the same region.

The main fault of these figures is apparent – they omit casualties during the actual round-up and deportation of the Tatars. Tatars speak of very heavy casualties on the trains, in some of which no food at all was available on journeys lasting (as the first MOOP letter implies) not less than eleven days, and often much more. Entire trains are reported as abandoning the journey after the death of all the deportees aboard.

This alone seems to make the Crimeans' own figure of 46·3 per cent in the probable range, even accepting the MOOP figures. In addition, the Crimeans claim to have arrived at it by a careful mutual census and registration.

If the Crimean Tatars suffered 46 per cent deaths in the first eighteen months, then (if this was roughly the proportion for the other deported nations, except the Volga Germans, for whom we may perhaps reduce it by half) we can take it that about 480,000 died in the seven earlier operations, to which must be added the 50,000 Meskhetian dead, to make 530,000. And the census seems to support this. As can be seen, the 1959 total figures for the Chechens, Ingushi, Karachai, Balkars and Kalmyks altogether, assuming them to be correct, are within less than 1 per cent of the 1939 ones, while the total population of the USSR has gone up by over 22 per cent in the same period.

Clearly, even allowing for the special advantages of recuperation found in polygamous races, casualties have been enormous. And when we are specifically assured that it was largely among the old and the very young that the first wave of deaths took place – i.e., those who would least affect the birth rate – we may feel that fuller investigation, were it possible, might show a casualty figure at least as high as and perhaps higher than the one we have advanced. As so often, this must await more official, or rather more authentic, figures from the USSR.

It must be said that there are still a number of anomalies in the 1959 census, as it applies to the deported nations. First, although it took place after the date announced for the return of the Kalmyks, Karachai and Balkars, it only lists in their newly reconstituted Republic and Provinces 64,882 Kalmyks, 67,830 Karachai and 34,088 Balkars. Moreover, the remainder are not given in the otherwise very exhaustive nationality lists of other parts of the RSFSR or the Central Asian Republics; nor are those Chechens and Ingushi not yet in their republic. (There is one peculiar exception – 551 Kalmyks in the Agin-Buryat National Okrug.) This may seem to cast a certain doubt on the census figures. There seem some grounds for imagining that in the Kalmyk case in particular, as we have seen in our discussion of their anomalous treatment over the status of their territory in 1957–8, the total as given is larger than a strict interpretation would justify.

SOME FURTHER REWRITING

In the Khrushchev period the extremes of cultural Russification were modified a little. In 1954–6 the question of Tsarist conquest in general again became slightly controversial. And Shamil's case was at the centre of the controversy. At first it began to be cautiously maintained that Shamil's position could not be defined purely in terms of his being an 'Anglo-Turkish agent'. Then, at the end of 1955 and beginning of 1956, the question became bound up with a more general campaign against the old Stalinist falsifications which was conducted by the magazine *Voprosy Istorii* and its assistant editor Burdzhalov – encouraged by a sharp public attack by Mikoyan at the Twentieth Party Congress on certain Stalinist works of history. A stroke of luck for the rehabilitators was that it happened to have been Bagirov who had acted as Stalin's mouthpiece in attacking Shamil. He had fallen with Beria, and his execution was announced in April 1956. His statements could thus be freely attacked and no one could defend them.

A conference of readers of *Voprosy Istorii* held in Moscow, 25–8 January 1956, was the scene of a formal attempt to rehabilitate Shamil. A. M. Pikman spoke strongly for the pro-Shamil view, making the obvious enough point that those who shared his views 'for several years did not have the opportunity of stating their case in the press'.[1] Pikman, evidently with the support of Burdzhalov, followed this by an article forthrightly putting the case for Shamil and the Mountaineers.[2] Burdzhalov's campaign met with immediate resistance. A party historian wrote revealingly[3] that he deplored the re-evaluation of Shamil because 'it would not further the strengthening of friendship among the nationalities' of the Soviet Union. But for the moment at least the pro-Shamil historians had latitude to put their views forward.

Pikman's views were again strongly attacked in an article by Bushuev,[4] who even asserted of the long and bitter Shamil wars that 'the incorporation of the Caucasus in Russia was of exceptional importance . . . in the history of the (eventually) friendly Russo-Caucasian relations'. But the same issue carried reports of two conferences on the Shamil Question held at Makhachkala in Daghestan in October and at the Academy of Sciences in Moscow in November. At these the official line, put by N. A. Smirnov, A. V. Fadeev and others, conceded the anti-colonial aspect of the Mountaineers' resistance, but stressed the reactionary character of Muridism and the importance of Anglo-Turkish imperialist support. A few speakers put forward an even more strongly anti-Shamil view. But the great majority took a stand favourable to the Imam and his followers on all counts. Burdzhalov declared flatly, 'The Mountaineers were fighting for their freedom and independence . . . what took place was not unification but conquest.' I. Lavrov said it was a mistake to 'approach history like politics projected into the past; we need science which reveals the objective truth. In the struggle of the Mountaineers the main thing is their struggle for freedom.' M. A. Mamakaev called the Turkish issue a red herring. 'The Mountaineers . . . wanted neither the knout of Nicholas I nor the noose of the Janissaries: the Mountaineers were seeking their own freedom and independence.' A. A. Abilov went to the length of recalling that the Bolsheviks only obtained Mountaineer support in the Revolution by appealing to the Shamil tradition.

At about this time, too, the Bureau of the Daghestan Communist Party repudiated a resolution it had made in support of the Stalin–Bagirov view of Shamil in August 1950. It issued orders for materials on Shamil to be restored to local libraries and museums, and called for historical re-evaluation of events such as the rebellion of 1877.

The Shamil issue had in any case become entangled with the whole question of 'liberalization' in historiography. Burdzhalov had taken the decisions of the Twentieth Party Congress in

February 1956 as permission to historians to seek out and publish the facts, to tell the truth as they saw it, and to maintain a variety of viewpoints. This was, as it soon appeared, a mis-interpretation of the decrees of the Party leadership. Burd-zhalov's own troubles were mainly due to his publishing un-suitable facts and inferences about the events of 1917 in Petrograd. The official counter-attack was an unsigned article 'Observe Strictly the Leninist Principle of "Partiinost" in Historical Science' which appeared in the dominating Party journal *Kommunist* (No. 4, 1957). This asserted that 'no one among serious Soviet scholars casts doubt on the progressive nature of the unification of the peoples of the Northern Caucasus with Russia'. It attacked Pikman and *Voprosy Istorii* as follows:

> The impression is generally formed that *Voprosy Istorii* sometimes uses the discussion section not in order to organize truly useful scientific discussions but to impose upon the readers its own biased viewpoint. A case in point is A. M. Pikman's article on Shamil's movement (No. 3, 1956), clamorous in tone, weak in argumentation, ignoring the level of scientific knowledge already attained.
>
> The author is 'diverted' from an analysis of the social structure of mountain society in the nineteenth century and from a class analysis of the movement itself. . . . A. Pikman justifies the religious-political system of the Imamate as allegedly being the inevitable and only possible form for an effective fight by the mountaineers against the Tsarist colonizers. In regard to the efforts by Britain and Turkey to use Shamil's movement for expansionist purposes, he is inclined to deny them altogether, seeing in this merely a perfectly justified effort by the mountaineers to seek support from anybody anywhere. He depicts Shamil as a champion of democracy, and tries to prove that it was only because of the weakness of the movement that Shamil 'was unable to establish a genuinely democratic administration'. The author of the article overlooks the fact that the movement led by Shamil developed on a basis of semi-patriarchal, semi-feudal

relationships, and that Muridism became the ideology of the militant feudal and clerical nobility.

At the same time it granted an 'anti-colonialist' element to Shamil's movement, and conceded that he was not an Anglo-Turkish agent pure and simple.

By the previous issue of *Voprosy Istorii*, its editorial board had lost seven of its previous members, including Burdzhalov. Smirnov, who had maintained an essentially anti-Shamil position, retained his post. Later issues of the periodical attacked Burdzhalov on various matters and Pikman for his Caucasian views.

The 1956–7 controversy about Shamil, which established the line that is still valid, seems to show various things. First, the majority of historians, and in particular those of the North Caucasus itself, favour an interpretation of the Shamil movement in terms of its progressive national-liberation character, which also accords with proto-Marxist views. The Party leadership, on the other hand, seeks the imposition of a single 'scientific' estimate – which is to say, as with previous attitudes so described, one which is in accord with the political tactics of the moment. The extremes of repression and Russification which marked Stalin's last years are abandoned, by an extension natural in Soviet circumstances, as much in the case of the dead Shamil as of the living Chechens. The national hero is no longer to be smeared as a venal traitor. His movement's motives are admitted to be honourable. On the other hand there is no reversion to pre-Stalinist views about the essentially progressive nature of the Mountaineers' struggle. With all the new concessions to local feeling, the essential is not conceded: nothing that justifies independence from Russia, in 1860 or 1970, is to be tolerated. Nor can Shamil's 'ideology', with its egalitarian-religious context, be treated with anything but hostility – though it must be as Muridist rather than Islamic that it is condemned. On this last point Pikman had been particularly awkward, blurting out the unfortunate fact that

> no special religious sect called Muridism existed at that period either in the Caucasus or in Turkey. One can talk about

Islam as a religion but not about a special Muridist ideology. Under the guise of criticizing non-existent Muridism the general dogmas of Mohammedanism, allegedly many times worse than those of Christianity, are being criticized.[5]

It should be remarked that in their campaign in favour of the facts of history Burdzhalov and his colleagues carried the 'liberal' line much further than operators in any other field, except for some novelists and poets. The argument about Shamil was only one of many issues on which 1956 saw a struggle between the historians and the temporarily confused Department of Agitation and Propaganda of the Central Committee. *Voprosy Istorii* was much more sharply attacked for its attitude to Party history, and in the winter of 1956–7 the heavy guns of not only *Kommunist*, but *Partiinaya Zhizn* and *Pravda* itself, were brought to bear on the little fortress of objectivity, which was finally silenced. (The way in which these shifts in officially promulgated truth affect even loyal Communists was strikingly illustrated in an extraordinary apology, and expression of shame, by the Avar poet, Rasul Gamzatov, for contradictory verses on Shamil which he had written in 1951 and 1961 respectively.[6])

For the Party the Shamil issue clearly represented the National Question pure and simple. And if the present solution (whereby both the Mountaineers and their conquerors were in a way fighting for progress, but the latter more so) is an illogical and shaky sort of compromise, the policy behind it is equally so. The present tendency seems to be to say as little as possible about the facts of Caucasian history, and to confine comment to very occasional repetition of the formula arrived at. The difficulties produced by the following up of the attack on Stalin with a very large measure of back-pedalling is even more acute in Party history. For instance, there has now been, for fourteen years, *no* official story at all, plausible or otherwise, about the rights and wrongs of the 1936–8 trials. Any further historical rewriting awaits political developments, and this applies to Shamil too.

In general we may take the changes in the Soviet attitude to

Shamil as illustrative of the whole progress of Communist nationality policy. In the earlier years of the regime everything was done to harness the whole immense prestige of the Imam to the service of the government: the national freedom he had fought for, it was alleged, had been attained by his Soviet successors. When it had become obvious that the nationalities had ceased to see the Soviet Union as answering their desire for independence, Shamil was denounced: as a symbol of resistance to Moscow rule, he was too exciting to the local population. Yet, as the post-Stalin regime seems to have felt, to forfeit this powerful symbolic figure to the enemy meant a dead loss, an admission that the nationalities could only be ruled by Russification and brute force. The present attitude can be seen as an attempt to make the best of the national traditions of the Mountaineers, insofar as that is compatible with preserving the essence of the Stalinist position – which sees 'unification with Russia', in Shamil's time and now, as the overriding *summum bonum*.

As to post-rehabilitation *Encyclopaedia* and other articles on the deported peoples, in general it may be said that they return, though only up to a point, to the views of the pre-deportation first edition, thus bringing these people's official history in line once more with that of other Soviet minorities.

The Chechen-Ingush ASSR article, which may again be taken as typical, starts with a long summary of what appears to be admirable research work done since the first edition (which said that 'almost nothing is known' of the peoples' history before the seventeenth century) into earlier times. Identifications are made with tribes mentioned by Strabo and Armenian writers, and it is concluded on these and archaeological grounds that the Chechen-Ingushi are 'aborigines of the North Caucasus'.

The gradual conversion to Islam, starting in the seventeenth century, the first clash with Russia in 1732, the rise of Urshuma, are detailed. Then come the Murids. 'The movement of the Mountaineers, clothed in the religious cloak of reactionary Muridism, had deep social and economic reasons.' Shamil, 'by cruel methods succeeded in breaking the resistance of the feudalists of Daghestan . . . and united tens of varilingual tribes of Mountaineers into one state unity.' He was defeated because the Tsar was stronger, but also because

> in Shamil's movement itself were lodged insoluble internal contradictions. While annihilating the Avar Khans, and professing the equality of all Muslims before the Shariya, Shamil in the long run created a new feudalizing autocracy in the persons of the naibs and other officials, which oppressed the people no less than the Russian generals and officials.

This resulted in a popular movement for peace with Russia. Tsarist oppression is described in strong terms, but 'at the same time, the unification of Chechniya and Russia promoted the economic and social development of the Chechen-Ingush people'.

In the Revolution Soviet power was established in Chechniya 'amid great difficulties, fierce class war, bloody battles'. Afterwards struggles against the kulaks, who used religious and national propaganda, and 'a stubborn struggle to liquidate' the Shariya, are described. And we are back with the remarks about national satisfaction which appeared in the first edition. They read even more peculiarly in retrospect, after the deportation, than in prospect. For instance it might seem, in the circumstances, to require a little nerve to write: 'Soviet power freed the toiling masses of Checheno-Ingushetia from national oppression and liquidated national inequality.'

The historical section of the article consists of approximately two and a half pages from earliest times up to the Revolution, one page from the Revolution till 1920, half a page from 1920 to 1939 and a quarter of a column from 1939 to 1957. The events of the war are given as that 'the toilers of the Chechen-Ingush ASSR reconstructed their economy and actively assisted the front', that the Germans reached the area but were defeated, and that in 1944 5,000 Chechen and Ingush workers were in jobs in oil and other undertakings in Grozny.

Later happenings are presented as follows:

> In 1944 the Chechen-Ingush ASSR was liquidated. In accordance with a decree of the Presidium of the Supreme Soviet of the USSR of 9 January 1957 the Chechen-Ingush ASSR was re-established.

There is also a cultural portion which mentions the appearance in 1956, in Kazakhstan and Kirgizia, of two collections of Chechen literature, and says that in 1957 a conference of Chechen-Ingush writers was called, to 'define new tasks before the national literature'.

The other articles are similar. That on the Karachai-Cherkess AP mentions as one of the characteristics of Tsarist colonialism that 'Russian officials sat in the administrative apparatus and the courts'. It does not refer to the liquidation of the Karachai AP at all, giving simply the administrative change of 9 January 1957.

That on Kalmykia describes the Tsarist oppressions of the nineteenth century very clearly. After the Revolution 'bandit detachments recruited by feudal, kulak and nationalist elements' were liquidated, and then the kulaks, who 'offered bitter resistance'. The liquidation of the Kalmyk republic itself is mentioned in the same terms as in the Chechen-Ingush article. The culture section reveals that a paper in Russian and Kalmyk (*Halumg Unn* – *Sovietskaya Kalmykia*) is coming out in Elista. A collection *Light on the Steppes* has been published, and in general 'the national and social renaissance of the Kalmyk people began after the victory of the great October Socialist Revolution'.

The articles on the peoples as such are brief and mainly about economy and folk crafts and arts. But it is also claimed that 'in Soviet times Balkar literature was created' and so on, and that the nations were backward until Soviet times. The religious affiliation of 'the believing section' of the nation is often given. And there is one revealing point on the Kalmyks: 'with the unification in kolkhozes, they became settled'.

The comparisons with the previous edition hardly need labouring. In general one may say that the present line is:

(*a*) to describe their resistance to Tsarism as well intentioned up to a point, but leading only to local despotism, to which 'unification' with Russia was preferable, on account of its progressive effects.

(*b*) to say little or nothing about recent unpleasantnesses.

(c) to claim the nations as grateful, and rightly grateful, to the Soviet system.

Quite apart from the unavoidable matter of the *Encyclopaedia*, other occasions began to occur in which something had to be said about the rehabilitated nations. The year 1957, for instance, was celebrated as the 400th anniversary of the accession of Kabarda to Russia. (In other countries, as Kolarz says, the anniversary of their independence is celebrated, but for the nations of the USSR it is the anniversary of their submission. In October 1957, the Karachai had to go through the same celebrations.) This event was celebrated with considerable pomp. One of the ceremonies was a meeting in the Kremlin, on 20 June 1957, at which the main speech was made by RSFSR First Vice-Premier Sapinov, who said that the Russian people 'has always been the reliable friend of the peoples of Kabarda and Balkaria'. This seemed to confirm that the official intention was to suppress, as far as possible, mention of some unpleasant facts.

In connection with the anniversary, *A History of Kabarda*, edited by N. A. Smirnov, was published by the Academy of Sciences of the USSR. There has been no recent history of the deported nations themselves, and this work on the Kabardines might be expected to give us more information both as to the facts and as to the attitude of the Soviet authorities than any similar work. For the Kabardines had, while remaining in good odour themselves, been previously in administrative relations with the deported Balkars.

The book's references to the Balkars are comparatively few. It does indeed mention the 'historical relations' between Kabarda and Balkaria, and speaks of how the Kabardines and Balkars living in the mountains had been connected by the movements of flocks of each to the area of the other during the relevant seasons.

Though the only political figure with a photograph in the book is Stalin, the general tone is on the whole more objective than those of the Stalin period, and it takes the present line that although the resistance movements against the Tsarist annexation were reactionary, they nevertheless had national resistance characteristics.

This objectivity becomes less and less noticeable as we reach the time of the 1917 revolution, and more particularly in the years after that event. We are, however, told certain once suppressed facts: that in January 1921 a Decree of the All-Russian Central Executive Committee set up the Mountain ASSR, including 'Kabarda, Balkaria, Ossetia, Chechniya, Ingushetia', etc. It is admitted that 'Kulak banditism' resulted as late as 1921 in a state of war being declared in Kabarda.

The later administrative history of the territory is correctly described, Balkars and all: in September 1921, the setting up of a Kabardine autonomous province; in 1922 the inclusion of Balkaria in the province, and its renaming as Kabardine-Balkar Autonomous Province; and the setting up in 1937 of a Kabardine-Balkar ASSR. On several occasions the whole territory is referred to, even though the Balkars are not much treated separately. For instance 'the nations' of Kabardino-Balkaria are stated to have benefited from a complete cultural revolution in the thirties. It is stated that on 12 September 1937, in the elections to the Supreme Soviet of the USSR, 'in the whole Republic 98.6 per cent of the electors took part in the voting. Of this number 99.7 per cent voted for the candidate of the bloc of Communists and non-party men in the Supreme Soviet, and 99.5 per cent for the Soviet of nationalities.' That is, the Balkars, who were to be shown as mass traitors, were virtually unanimous in the election. Similar (indeed better) results were obtained in the elections for the Supreme Soviet of the Republic in June 1938 – 99.9 per cent of the electors voted, and of these 99.95 per cent voted for the Party list.

The most interesting part of the history of the territory would have been an account of what precisely caused the trouble with the Balkars in the war, followed by the circumstances of their deportation and of their return, together with an estimate of their present numbers. Although sixty-two pages deal with the period in question, these facts do not emerge. But, still, there are signs of unsatisfactory co-operation.

To weaken the resistance of the Caucasian nations Fascist propaganda spread rumours about special peaceful connections between Fascist Germany and the mountaineers, made efforts to divide the Russians and the mountaineers, and sowed national dissension.

The Germans, who occupied the territory for from two to five months, are stated to have been strongly resisted. But again, in October 1942 the Provincial Committee of the Party

uncovered errors and inadequacies in the work of the provincial and regional Party organizations, including the leadership of the partisan movement in the regions of the republic occupied by the enemy, which expressed themselves in inadequate struggle against bourgeois nationalist elements, in the service of the Hitlerite occupiers.

The Germans are said to have brought back princes, kulaks and others driven out by the revolution and some attempt is made to imply that these were the main offenders. Among the crimes of the Germans and 'their bourgeois nationalist lackeys' the fact that 'they annihilated the kolkhozes and sovkhozes' is prominently stated. Much is made of the partisan movement, but most of its named members appear to be Russians, and its 'faults' included the fact that it did not organize bases in the rear of the enemy, but only infiltrated from time to time from behind the Soviet Army's lines.

By January 1943 the Republic had been entirely liberated, and a great deal of detail is given about economic and other measures. Here again the working people 'of the whole Republic actively took part'. And they 'voluntarily' subscribed to loans and to special levies for equipping forces. Politically it is said that 'the Central Committee of the Party approved the work of the Provincial Committee', but again mentioned certain 'errors and insufficiencies'.

The Central Committee considered that, although the bourgeous nationalist elements had been struck a blow in the first period after the driving out of the German Fascist occupiers, there were still in the Republic facts showing

> bourgeois nationalist ideology, and also the revival of private
> property moods

and other lesser troubles. Finally the deportation of the Balkars
is described and condemned as follows:

> In 1944 the Kabardine-Balkar ASSR was changed into the
> Kabardine ASSR in connection with the fact that at the end
> of 1943 and beginning of 1944 all the Balkars were deported
> without reason from the territory of the Republic. This re-
> pressive measure, carried out in connection with the whole
> people, constituted a crude breach of socialist legality and of
> Leninist principles of national policy.

In 1945 the twenty-fifth anniversary of Kabardine autonomy
was celebrated, and thereafter several chapters deal with
economic and cultural progress. In 1954 and 1955, it is added,
99 per cent of the electors once again voted for the Party list in
the national and local elections. Finally,

> The Central Committee of the Communist Party and the
> Government of the USSR, in connection with the decisions
> of the Twentieth Congress of the CPSU, put into effect
> measures to rehabilitate the Balkar nation and the correction
> of the injustices carried out in connection with it. In February
> 1957, the session of the Supreme Soviet confirmed a decree
> of the Presidium of the Supreme Soviet of the USSR on the
> restoration of the national autonomy of the Balkar nation, and
> the renaming of the Kabardine ASSR the Kabardine-Balkar
> ASSR. Practical measures for the reconstruction of the Repub-
> lic were made the responsibility of the Council of Ministers of
> the KB ASSR, together with representatives of the Balkar
> nation. The Kabardine nation, for many years in comrade-
> ship and brotherhood with the Balkar people, heartily ap-
> proved this just decision.

A few other publications of the period, mainly cultural, deal
with the rehabilitated nations, and in a curious manner. For
example, a book on minority musical culture covered the
Kabardine-Balkar and Chechen-Ingush ASSRs.[7] In both cases

a considerable amount of historical background is given, but without any reference to the deportation. The Balkars, like the Kabardines, are said to have been allowed to remain in economic and cultural backwardness by Tsarist Russia:

> Soviet Kabardino-Balkaria shows itself in present times as a flourishing area, where with every year socialist industry and village economy equipped with advanced technique grows stronger .... A Kabardine-Balkar culture, socialist in content and national in form, thrives and develops.

The Balkars are described as 'tenacious, bold, rough and hardworking', as a result of their mountain life. Their attachment to the Soviet state, in the past as well as now, is demonstrated by the fact that 'the events connected with the Great October Revolution found a most convincing echo in the creations of the Balkar people'. As an example songs are given (dated 1940, 1941, 1957) in praise of Kirov, of the Party and Komsomol, and of Lenin. The last is quoted: 'Lenin gave us the Party, and the Party brought the poor folk to freedom and happiness.' It is also noted that much of Balkar popular creation is concerned with

> Kolkhoz songs and songs of the new life. The old customs are disappearing with the centuries-old prejudices. The new, healthy life is supplanting outworn connections.

Incidentally the poet Kazim Mechaes, described as 'the founder of Balkar literature', is mentioned as dying in 1945, but where and how is not stated. He was, in fact, a victim of the deportation.

The article (by N. Rechmensky) on the Chechen-Ingush ASSR's music is the only one with which there are no photographs of artistic activities (those of the Kabardine-Balkar ASSR appear to be all of Kabardines). A description of the agrarian and other riches of the republic is followed by a historical sketch beginning, 'The history of the Chechens and Ingushi, these freedom-loving and warrior peoples, has been little studied and still awaits its researchers.' It mentions the legendary origins, contact with Russia, Tsarist conquest, popular movements under Mansur, Shamil and others, to the time when the Revolution ended the 'persecutions and oppressions which the Chechens and Ingushi suffered at the hand of the colonizers'. The Revolution brought 'complete liberation from centuries of slavery'. Both peoples fought heroically against the White Guards in the Civil War. Of their history since 1917 only this is said:

> There was much change in the life and existence of the Chechens and Ingushi after the victory of October. Serious attention was paid to questions of culture and the education of the people. Art gained unlimited opportunities for development.

Some of the resulting songs are quoted. For instance, there is one song of 'Ingush maidens' which runs as follows:

> The Tsar-enemy kept the workers in darkness.
> But they won justice in heroic struggle.
> Soviet people, Ingushi, know
> How the workers gained your rights.
> We will construct a new life,
> We will strengthen the kolkhozes.
> We will fulfil the five-year plan in three years.

Songs to Lenin are also quoted, and a longer Chechen song about the October Revolution, as a result of which,

> We abolished the old laws,
> A happy youth grows in our land . . . .
> The Communist Party goes from victory to victory,
> It increases the sowing of the kolkhoz fields,
> It defeats the enemy, standing in the way,
> It uproots the concealed traitor.

The Chechens and Ingushi finally are again said to be 'constructing their own culture, socialist in content and national in form, in the fraternal family of the peoples of the soviet socialist republics'. And that is all.

This sort of treatment of the rehabilitated nations is more or less typical of what began to be the constant line in Soviet publications. It seems particularly inadequate and unconvincing. In effect, the same is said about the Chechens or the Balkars as used to appear in Soviet propaganda in the period before the war. Their cultural and political situation is represented as splendid and their devotion to the Soviet regime as immense. This was evidently untrue before the war, and it would strain anyone's credulity to imagine that loyalty and contentment have increased as a result of the experiences of the past years. Moreover, the simple hushing up of those injustices is grotesque: no one would expect the Soviet rulers, especially in their present mood, to dwell on the deportations much, but what good can come of insulting the intelligence of readers by such *suppressio veri*, combined with the obvious *suggestio falsi* implied by the remarks actually made about the peoples concerned? In general, such an attitude to truth and to objective history (of which these are by no means the only examples) is bound to make all observers uneasy. It is obviously dangerous for all of us when a great state is ruled by men for whom a Party decision displaces a fact.

12

NATIONS STILL IN EXILE

WITH all the restitution that took place it cannot fail to be remarked that two of the suppressed republics failed to re-emerge. Of the eight deported nations three resumed their old constitutional status. One has been downgraded; one was downgraded for a time then restored to its old status; and three others, numbering over three-quarters of a million, were only slowly and incompletely rehabilitated, without regaining their lands.

Quite early on there were references to Germans in Siberia. These may in any given case be the ones settled there already and not the deportees from European Russia. But the whole German minority, even in Siberia, was victimized, and even such reports have some significance. For example, a decree of the Supreme Soviet of 5 April 1951, making awards to collective farmers, includes a number from farms with German names in the Omsk province (such as *Arbeiter* and *Rosa Luxemburg*).

Later reports almost certainly referred to deportees. For example *Kazakhstanskaya Pravda* of 7 June 1955 listed the champion dairy-maids of the Republic over the period October 1954 to May 1955. Of the twenty-one names from the Kokchetav, Pavlodar and Semipalatinsk Provinces seventeen were German, while there were four more, apparently German, elsewhere in the Republic, including two out of six names in Karaganda.

Kazakhstanskaya Pravda of 16 June 1955 gave the champion milk-maids of the State Farms. The German names were one out of three in Kustanai, two out of three in Semipalatinsk, two out of four in South Kazakhstan and two out of two in Kokchetav. These figures probably give a reasonable idea of where the Germans were most highly concentrated in Kazakhstan. They also indicate that the German population on the whole was at least farming under conditions no worse than those of the remainder of the population. In view of the generally superior reputation for livestock and stud-farming of the Soviet Germans, the figures probably should not be thought of as being any indication of the proportion of Germans to the rest of the population. That their civil rights were not, then at least, respected in the same way as their farming abilities, seems clear. A list was published in *Kazakhstanskaya Pravda* of 11 March 1955 of deputies elected to the Kazakh Supreme Soviet on 6 March 1955. This list showed three doubtful names: Fedor Efremovich German, Dmitri Ivanovich Berlin and Alexei Andreevich Pak, which may be of German, Jewish or Baltic origin – though Pak is more probably a Korean. (The Christian names are Russian.) Apart from these three doubtfuls there were no Germans among the 425 names listed.

Yet the farm awards showed some progress. And it seems that towards the end of 1955, when the general decision on rehabilitation for the Chechens and others was evidently taken, the Soviet leaders definitely decided to grant a measure of relief to the Germans, though in their case a measure far short of full restitution. No doubt for this reason, the decision was not given publicly. But a decree of the Presidium of the Supreme Soviet (one of the many which, as we have seen, do not easily reach the public eye) is reported in the following terms:

Decree of the Presidium of the Supreme Soviet of the USSR of 13 December 1955 – On the Revocation of the Restrictions in the Legal Position of Germans and their family dependants now in conditions of Special Settlement:

Considering the fact that the existing restrictions in the legal position of German special settlers and members of their families, who were deported to various regions of the country, are no longer necessary in future, the Presidium of the Supreme Soviet of the USSR decides:

1. Germans and members of their families who at the

time of the Great Patriotic War were exiled to a Special Settlement are to be released from attachment to the Special Settlement and freed from the administrative control of the organs of the MVD. The same is valid for German citizens of the USSR who after their repatriation from Germany were put in a Special Settlement.

2. It is laid down that the revocation of the restrictions on the Germans connected with Special Settlement does not imply the return of the property confiscated in connection with the deportation, and further that they do not have the right to return to the regions from which they were deported.[1]

This throws considerable light on the legal and administrative status of the deported nations at the time of their exile (and the reference to the families, as apart from the Germans themselves, is worth noting, as seeming to imply that non-German wives of Germans suffered the fate of their husbands). On the limited nature of this rehabilitation, it speaks for itself. Above all they were in no way exculpated from the original charges. But further improvements in the Germans' conditions continued. For example, the Ministry of Education of the RSFSR issued an order on 9 April 1957 providing for their children to be taught in their own language.

One special effort was made in 1957 to track down a small section of the German minority. These are the Mennonites, a pacifist protestant sect which emigrated from Dutch and Rhineland territories in the eighteenth century, and were, like the other German immigrants, welcomed by the Tsars. Under the Tsars their pacifist principles were respected and they were allowed to join a special forest service instead of serving in the army. At the time of the Revolution there were about 100,000 of them. Among them, owing to their religious principles and practices, there was a total absence of class struggle. Moreover their religion was for them more important than their origins and they protested against inclusion in the 'German National Districts' in the areas where they lived.

Conscientious objection was abolished in Russia in the thirties on the grounds that no one wished any longer to make such objection. The Mennonites did. The resulting repressive measures were severe, and merged almost imperceptibly – via mass deportations of Mennonite males – into the general removal to Siberia of all the Russian Germans. During the war some contrived to escape through Germany to the West.

In 1957 the Soviet authorities allowed an American, Dr Binder, and a Canadian, Pastor Wiens, to visit their co-religionists. They searched for them throughout Soviet Asia and finally found rather less than half of the original population. None was in the Ukraine and about half of the survivors were in their old Siberian settlements. The remainder had been resettled, mainly in Kazakhstan and the Altai region. About a thousand of them formed a community in Karaganda, the great exile city in Kazakhstan. Visitors reported that no religious life had been possible for the community for more than twenty years, until 1954, and that they were no longer taught in their own language, so that the younger generation had been considerably Russified. (Only 75 per cent of those in the USSR registered as German in the 1959 census gave German as their 'mother tongue'.)

But some of the same sort of attention had now begun to be paid to the Germans, as targets of political work, as had been the case with the Chechens in 1955–6. *Kazakhstanskaya Pravda* of 7 June 1957 complained that 'mass political work was especially badly conducted in the native languages among the Uighur, German and Chechen-Ingush nationalities'. Again, in 1963, an ideological representative of the Kirgiz Central Committee complained that a section of the German population had remained outside the Party's influence, and that few of them joined the Party or the Komsomol, or took leading positions in the kolkhozes. As a result the Christian sects had gained considerable influence, and were 'a breeding-ground for nationalism'.[2]

In 1958 two newspapers in German started to appear in the Soviet Union – *Neues Leben* in Moscow and *Arbeit* in Barnaul, capital of the Altai Territory. This seemed to establish that the largest German settlements were in the Altai region, though most unofficial reports have referred to areas of the Altai on the steppe fairly distant from Barnaul itself. (One of the seventeen German National Districts existing in the USSR before the war, over and above the Volga Republic, had been in the Altai.) The original circulation announced for *Arbeit* was 6,500 copies. Its treatment of Germans in the USSR may be thought rather curious. It described the prowess of Soviet tractor drivers and others with German names, but did not refer overtly to the fact of their being German, nor describe the happy life of Germans in the USSR taken collectively. It also ran a useful and pathetic column through which Germans sought information about members of their families, often last seen fifteen or sixteen years previously. Its existence, and that of *Neues Leben*, is certainly an improvement. But before the war twenty-one German papers came out in the Volga Republic alone.

At the same time German-language broadcasts for Germans in the USSR began from Radio Moscow and Radio Alma Ata.

In 1964 a decree was published publicly rehabilitating the Volga Germans, but still not granting them the right to return to their old settlements. That is, the accusations were at last withdrawn, but the punishment remained in force! The decree ran as follows:

Decree of the Presidium of the USSR Supreme Soviet:
On introducing amendments into the decree of the Presidium of the USSR Supreme Soviet of 28 August 1941 'On Resettling the Germans Living in Districts Along the Volga'.

Accusations of actively helping the German-Fascist invaders and complicity with them were raised in the ukase of the USSR Supreme Soviet of 28 August 1941 'On Resettling the Germans Living in Districts Along the Volga' with respect to large groups of Germans who were Soviet citizens.

Life has shown that these indiscriminate accusations were unfounded and were an instance of arbitrariness during the period of the cult of Stalin's personality. In fact, during the Great Patriotic War, the overwhelming majority of the German population, together with the entire Soviet people, facilitated the victory of the Soviet Union over Fascist

Germany with their labour and in the postwar years actively participated in Communist construction.

Thanks to the great help of the Communist Party and the Soviet State, the German population has firmly taken root in its new places of residence in the years which have elapsed and enjoys all the rights of the USSR citizens. Soviet citizens of German nationality are conscientiously working at enterprises, sovkhozes, kolkhozes, and establishments and are actively participating in public and political life. Many of them are deputies to supreme or local Soviets of the RSFSR, Ukrainian, Kazakh, Uzbek, Kirgiz, and other Union Republics and hold leading posts in industry and agriculture and in the Soviet and Party apparatus. Thousands of Soviet German citizens have been awarded USSR decorations and medals for successes in labour and have honorary titles awarded by Union Republics. In the districts of a number of regions, territories and republics with a German population there are primary and secondary schools where instruction is carried out in the German language or where study of the German language has been organized for children of school age, and there are regular radio broadcasts and newspapers in German and other cultural activities are carried out for the German population.

The Presidium of the USSR Supreme Soviet decrees:

1. To abrogate the part of the ukase of the Presidium of the USSR Supreme Soviet of 28 August 1941 'On Resettling the Germans Living in Districts Along the Volga' (Protocol of the Session of the Presidium of the USSR Supreme Soviet, 1941, No. 9, art. 256) which contains sweeping accusations against the German population living in districts along the Volga.

2. Considering the fact that the German population has taken root in its new place of residence on the territories of a number of republics, territories and regions of the country, whereas the districts where it formerly resided have been settled, the Councils of Ministers of Union Republics are instructed, with the aim of further developing areas with a German population, to continue rendering help and assistance

in economic and cultural construction to the German population living on the territory of their republics, taking their
national peculiarities and interests into consideration.

Chairman of the Presidium of the
USSR Supreme Soviet,
A. Mikoyan
Secretary of the Presidium of the
USSR Supreme Soviet,
M. Georgadze

Moscow, the Kremlin, 29 August 1964[3]

From its timing this rehabilitation seems to have been
connected with Khrushchev's effort to secure a détente with
West Germany. But it was ratified, if rather belatedly, after
Khrushchev's fall.

The present position of the Germans seems to be a difficult
one. Supporters of the movement for restoring the rights of the
Crimean Tatars imply that the situation of the Germans is the
worse of the two, at least when it comes to pressing for the
return to their old status (see p. 206).

In the late 1950s there were a few references to the Crimean
Tatars in the Soviet Press – in *Literaturnaya Gazeta, Druzhba
Narodov* and elsewhere.

As with the Germans, an unpublished decree of the Presidium of the Supreme Soviet in 1955 is quoted to the effect
that the Crimean Tatars were

1. Removed from conditions of Special Settlement, and
freed from the control of the MVD.

2. But 'that the removal from Special Settlement of the
persons covered in Article 1 of this Decree, does not carry
the right to the return of the property confiscated at the
deportation, and that they do not have the right to return to
the places from which they were deported.'

Rumours that some were allowed to return to the Crimea
seem to refer to a small-scale movement, apparently of border-
line cases partly of Russian or Ukrainian blood. Succeeding
editions of the handbook *U.S.S.R.: Territorial Administrative*

Divisions of the Union Republics carry appendixes showing changes of place name. Thus the Chechen Urus Martan is changed to Krasnoarmeiskoye in the 1954 edition, and this is reversed in the 1958 edition. Not all these changes are reversed, even in the Chechen case. For instance, the change of Novye Aldy to Chernorechiye remains. But what is more striking is that each edition carries a whole new series of changes in the Crimea, invariably from Turkic to Russian – Lenino, Sovietski, Belogorsk, and so on. What may be significant is the gradualness of the process. Though the population of the Crimea was already in 1959 little less than it was in 1939, it seems to be much more concentrated in the coastal strip and the towns, and appeals for settlers imply that much of the old Tatar land was only gradually being repopulated. On this view the villages would be receiving Russian names as they were resettled by Russians.

It was not until 1967 that a decree actually withdrawing the accusations against the Crimean Tatars, last of those originally accused, was promulgated.

Decree of the Presidium of the Supreme Soviet of the USSR
On citizens of Tatar nationality formerly resident
in the Crimea

After the liberation of the Crimea from Fascist occupation in 1944, accusations of the active collaboration of a section of the Tatars resident in the Crimea with the German usurpers were groundlessly levelled at the whole Tatar population of the Crimea. These indiscriminate accusations in respect of all the citizens of Tatar nationality who lived in the Crimea must be withdrawn, the more so since a new generation of people has entered on its working and political life.

The Presidium of the USSR Supreme Soviet decrees to:

1. Annul the section of the relevant decisions of State organs which contains indiscriminate accusations with respect to citizens of Tatar nationality who lived in the Crimea.

2. Note that the Tatars formerly living in the Crimea have taken root in the territory of the Uzbek and other Union Republics, they enjoy all the rights of Soviet citizens, take

part in public and political life, are elected deputies of the Supreme Soviets and local Soviets of deputies of working people, work in responsible posts in Soviet, economic and Party organs, radio broadcasts are made for them, a newspaper in their national language is published and other cultural measures are undertaken.

With the aim of further developing areas with Tatar population, the Councils of Ministers of Union Republics are instructed to continue rendering help and assistance to citizens of Tatar nationality in economic and cultural construction, taking account of their national interests and peculiarities.

Chairman of the Presidium of the
USSR Supreme Soviet,
N. Podgorny
Secretary of the Presidium of the
USSR Supreme Soviet,
M. Georgadze

Moscow, the Kremlin, 5 September 1967[4]

But it will be seen that, like the Volga Germans, the withdrawal of the accusations against the Crimean Tatars (or rather, in this case, against most of them) was not accompanied by an abrogation of the official penalties. Since 1967 the struggle of this small nation for the right to return to its homeland has been one of the central issues in the whole of the liberal resistance to ever-increasing Stalinization.

The restoration of the right to printing in the Crimean Tatar language is a notable advance on the position in which, even the previous year, this was described as an 'unwritten language', whose speakers used Kazakh or Uzbek for literary purposes.[5]

Lastly, an unpublished decree of the Supreme Soviet of 31 October 1956 freed the Meskhetians from MVD control, without giving them the right to return home, or to recover confiscated property. Over the next two years they made repeated applications to be allowed to resume their ancestral territory. The head of the Georgian KGB, Alexei Inauri,

replied to a mass petition that this could not be permitted.
Some were allowed to go to Azerbaidzhan, but no nearer.
Here they were settled on the Mugan Steppe, near the Caspian,
200–300 miles from Meskhetia. The bulk remained in Uzbekistan, but the scattered groups kept in touch.

In February 1964, a general meeting of the Meskhetian
national movement took place at a kolkhoz in the Tashkent
province. An Organizing Committee headed by the historian
Enver Odabashev-Khozravanadze was elected, and delega-
tions were sent to Moscow and Tbilisi. Again they were rebuffed
by both the Soviet and the Georgian authorities, and by the
Georgian KGB. Arrests followed.[6]

In June 1968 the Supreme Soviet issued the following decree
on the rehabilitation of the Meskhetian peoples, or rather
(since no accusations had been levelled at them) on their
restoration to civic equality:

Decree of the Presidium of the USSR Supreme Soviet
On the procedure of applying Article 2 of the ukase of the
Presidium of the USSR Supreme Soviet of 28 April 1956 and
Article 2 of the ukase of the Presidium of the USSR Supreme
Soviet of 31 October 1957 with regard to the following USSR
citizens – Turks, Kurds, Khemshils and Azerbaidzhanis,
formerly resident in the Georgian SSR.

The Presidium of the USSR Supreme Soviet decrees:

1. To make the interpretation that Turks, Kurds, Khemshils and Azerbaidzhanis who are USSR citizens and who
previously lived in the Adzhar ASSR, the Akhaltsikhe,
Akhalkalaki, Adigeni, Aspindza and Bogdanovka districts
of the Georgian SSR, and members of their families, enjoy
the same right as do all citizens of the Soviet Union to live
anywhere in the USSR in accordance with the legislation in
force on labour and passport regulations.

2. To note that citizens of Turkish and Kurdish nationality, Khemshils and Azerbaidzhanis who previously lived in
the Georgian SSR have settled permanently in the territory of
the Uzbek SSR, the Kazakh SSR and other Union Republics,
that they enjoy all the rights of Soviet citizens, take part in

public and political life and are elected to membership in Soviet, Party and Trade Union organs and that many of them have been awarded decorations and medals for successes in labour and have honorary titles.

To instruct the Councils of Ministers of the Union Republics in which the above-mentioned citizens live at present to continue to render them help and assistance in economic and cultural construction, taking their national interests and peculiarities into account.

Chairman of the Presidium of the
USSR Supreme Soviet,
N. Podgorny
Secretary of the Presidium of the
USSR Supreme Soviet,
M. Georgadze

Moscow, the Kremlin, 30 May 1968[7]

It will be seen that this decree is in the same terms as that on the Crimean Tatars. That is, it recognizes their civil rights but asserts that they have settled 'permanently' outside their homelands. As a result the Meskhetian 'national movement', which now completely united these formerly rather diverse groups, started a new agitation, like the Tatars, for their right to return home. But they, like the Tatars – indeed, even more than the Tatars – come from a strategically sensitive area.

After various fruitless appeals, a large number of delegates finally reached Tbilisi in July 1968, and on 26 July the Georgian First Secretary, Mzhavanadze, received a group of them. He told them that there was no longer any room for them in Meskhetia, but that a hundred families a year might be absorbed in other regions of Georgia. Several times in these proceedings the delegates were told that the Government would soon settle the matter. But finally, in November 1968, a delegation was officially told in Moscow that their homeland was the Soviet Union, and they should be content to stay wherever they happened to be in it. An official rebuffed their complaints with, 'I won't send your documents to Comrade Brezhnev, and he won't receive you. Go home and work.'[8]

13

RESPONSIBILITIES

PART of this book simply gives the early historical background of the nations deported. The remainder deals with their experience under Soviet rule and with the Soviet theory of how nationalities should be treated. The material for this part is based firmly, if not exclusively, on Soviet official documents. Nor is the non-Soviet evidence, striking though it is, essential to the argument: it merely illustrates and develops certain points.

It is perfectly true that this method of approach to Soviet documents in this sphere might be called selective. A round-up of everything that has been printed in the Soviet Union relevant to the minority question would probably show that 99 per cent of it consisted of accounts of progress and assertions of general contentment. Is it then unfair to have concentrated largely on the 1 per cent which does not?

The answer, of course, is, that if a thousand documents say that the minor nationalities of the USSR enjoy all the autonomy they wish and one document admits that most of those who had the opportunity were involved in mass efforts to overthrow the Soviet regime, then that one document refutes the 999 others and they are no longer worth studying except as examples of official propaganda. (In much the same way ninety-nine letters protesting innocence are unable to refute one fingerprint on the revolver.) It is true that certain of these documents appear more objective than others in that they give figures, indicating prosperity. This is not a book in which we can discuss the question of Soviet statistics at any length, but at least one can say that anyone who accepts them as they stand is probably inclined to be overly impressed by the mere fact that they are official. After all, a regime which falsifies the evidence in a show trial, as has been admitted, is quite capable of making up a set of figures. And previous chapters of this book have given examples of covert and overt falsification which may be sufficient to prove this point.

The relevance of the events in the North Caucasus and the Crimea to Soviet national policy as a whole seems clear. Of the non-Russian nationalities of the Soviet Union, the Germans reached or very closely approached the territories of two groups:

(1) the Estonians, Latvians, Lithuanians, Byelorussians and Ukrainians – the European and mainly Slav population of the border area, each of them forming an allegedly sovereign union republic and none numbering less than a million,

and

(2) the small nations of Asian origin in the southern fringe of the Slav lands: the Crimean Tatars, the Kalmyks, the Circassians (Cherkess and Adygei), the Karachai, the Balkars, the Kabardines, the Ossetians, the Chechens and the Ingushi. These small nations may be taken as a reasonably representative cross-section of the general Asian population of the USSR – mostly Mohammedan, though the Kalmyks are Buddhist. (The Ossetians are indeed more Christianized and Russianized than is largely typical.)

It will be seen that of the second group it was felt that six out of ten had proved not simply disloyal, but disloyal to the extent of mass treachery. There seems no reason to regard this as exceptional, and it may be taken as a plebiscite which would have given similar results if it had been held among any other of the USSR's minority groups. As to the largely European peoples in the first group, evidence of their opposition to Soviet rule and the fact that they took advantage of the German invasion to demonstrate it (though not necessarily in co-operation with the Germans – the Ukrainian 'Benderovtsy' seem to have fought both sides) is far greater than in the case of the Caucasian peoples. Deportation on an enormous scale took place among them, particularly in the Western Ukraine and in the Baltic States. Serov's next post, following on his assignment in the Crimea in June 1944, was to perform similar acts in Lithuania, with Suslov in political control. It appears that at least a million people were deported from the three Baltic states – a large number, though not of course the same as the attack in the Caucasus on entire nations. Yet practical, theoretical and propaganda difficulties rather than any lack of ill-will seem to have been all that stood in the way of the complete dispersion of these nations too. Khrushchev stated in his Secret Speech that the Ukrainians avoided meeting this fate only because there were too many of them and there was no place to which to deport them. Otherwise Stalin would have deported them also (a statement greeted with 'laughter and animation in the hall').

Khrushchev stated that blaming whole nations is contrary to Lenin's principles. If we accept this as self-evident, it must have been apparent to Khrushchev at the time of the deportations, though he does not claim that he made any protest. What is more to the point is that it must have been as apparent in 1953 after Stalin's death as it was three years later. Yet no action was taken to relieve this injustice until the later date. It can hardly be argued that it was necessary for the leaders to be gradual in reversing Stalin's 'errors'. For they carried out a major reversal almost immediately after his death. This was the repudiation of the alleged Doctors' Plot. This imaginary conspiracy was, according to Khrushchev, concocted by Stalin with the design of purging the top leaders of the Party. In fact, when it came to injustice directed against themselves they were quick enough to act. Injustice affecting over a million ordinary people does not seem to have struck them as in need of nearly such urgent attention.

Responsibility for the deportations rests in the first place with Stalin. Next we may rank those members of the Politbureau who voted for his proposal, either because they approved it, or because they preferred their own skins to those of a million other human beings. Beria, executed in 1953, may be presumed to have had some executive responsibility, both as Politbureau delegate in the Caucasian region earlier (during military operations there), and as head of the police ministries involved. Voroshilov is reported in overall charge of the Crimean operation. Suslov, who was Party Secretary in Stavropol at the relevant times, can probably be taken as concerned, at a lower level, in the recommendation and organization of at least the Karachai affair. Those immediately in charge were Ivan Serov, and his subordinates Gvishiani and Goglidze.

Goglidze was tried with Beria and shot in December 1953. Made Colonel-General in 1945 with other leading policemen, he had been a candidate member of the Central Committee of the Party since 1939. He was accused, with the others on trial, of a large number of crimes including acting as 'agents of international imperialism'. A number of inhuman persecutions were also alleged against him and the others, but these were all persecutions directed against important members of the Communist Party, and no reference was made to there having been anything wrong with his actions in the northern Caucasus. Kobulov, another of those shot with Beria, has been reported as concerned in the Crimean deportation. Another police official reported to have had a hand in the deportations, Kruglov, was Minister of the Interior from the fall of Beria until early in 1956, but has since sunk into obscurity. Gvishiani's fate remains doubtful. Reports of his execution have not been confirmed, and his son, who is married to Kosygin's daughter, holds a responsible position in Military Intelligence, which in Soviet conditions implies that his father was not a 'traitor'.

Serov himself became head of the KGB in 1954, and was transferred in 1959 to be head of Army Intelligence. He has since been removed, and there are reports of his expulsion from the Party in the last period of Khrushchev's rule, when a decree, dated 4 April 1962, cancelled the awards made on 8 March 1944 to the terror operatives. Voroshilov, removed from the Central Committee by Khrushchev, was reinstated by the present regime. Suslov is, of course, one of its leading members.

The Soviet Union seems by its attitude at the Nuremberg

G

War Crimes Trial to have committed itself to a refusal to accept as a defence for criminal acts that they were committed under orders. (Indeed the leaders openly rejected that defence in the case of another police official, Rodos – whose crime, however, was the maltreatment of leading Communists.) It seems reasonable to ask why Serov and others are not proceeded against. The signature by the Soviet Union of the United Nations Genocide Convention binds its government to prevent *and punish* it. It would seem that in principle there is a *prima facie* case for United Nations inquiry about that government's fulfilment of its obligations.

It may be relevant that, in his Secret Speech, Khrushchev concluded his catalogue of Stalin's crimes, including these deportations by saying:

> This question is complicated by the fact that all this which we have just discussed was done during Stalin's life under his leadership and with his concurrence; here Stalin was convinced that this was necessary for the defence of the interests of the working classes against the plotting of enemies and against the attack of the imperialist camp.
>
> He saw this from the position of the interest of the working class, of the interest of the labouring people, of the interest of the victory of socialism and communism. We cannot say that these were the deeds of a giddy despot. He considered that this should be done in the interest of the party, of the working masses, in the name of the defence of the revolution's gains. In this lies the whole tragedy!

This casts some sinister light on the whole matter. For it presents such things as these deportations as acts, judged after some years of consideration by the most critical of his successors erroneous, indeed, but yet capable of being committed in good faith by an honest Communist: mistakes due to misjudgment rather than tyranny.

The extent to which any feeling for the realities of nationalism had simply disappeared from the minds even of comparatively 'liberal' leading figures in the USSR may be seen from another passage in Khrushchev's Secret Speech. In it he condemns

Stalin for framing up certain party leaders in Georgia in the 'Mingrelian case'. These men had allegedly formed a nationalist organization to detach Georgia from the USSR. Khrushchev asked rhetorically if it were possible that nationalist tendencies had grown so great that there was any real danger of this. His answer is instructive:

> This is, of course, nonsense. It is impossible to imagine how such assumptions could enter anyone's mind. Everyone knows how Georgia has developed economically and culturally under Soviet rule.
>
> Industrial production of the Georgian Republic is 27 times greater than it was before the Revolution. Many new industries have arisen in Georgia which did not exist there before the Revolution: iron smelting, an oil industry, a machine-construction industry, etc. Illiteracy has long since been liquidated, which, in pre-Revolutionary Georgia, included 78 per cent of the population.
>
> Could the Georgians, comparing the situation in their republic with the hard situation of the working masses in Turkey, be aspiring to join Turkey? In 1955, Georgia produced 9 times as much electrical energy per person as Turkey. According to the available 1950 census, 65 per cent of Turkey's total population are illiterate, and, of the women, 80 per cent are illiterate. Georgia has 19 institutions of higher learning which have about 39,000 students; this is 8 times more than in Turkey (for each 1,000 inhabitants). The prosperity of the working people has grown tremendously in Georgia under Soviet rule.
>
> It is clear that, as the economy and culture develop, and as the socialist consciousness of the working masses in Georgia grows, the source from which bourgeois nationalism draws its strength evaporates.

It will be seen that on this view nationalism could not exist in Georgia because its industry was more highly developed than other countries in the Middle East. At its very best this is simply a crude form of paternalism.

Even if we allow the minor premise that the Georgian

masses are economically satisfied (and there is considerable reason to doubt this) the major premise is an astonishing piece of naïveté. National feeling has never been even in the slightest degree satisfied with foreign rule simply because it brings prosperity. To anyone who is not politically illiterate dozens of refutations will occur at once.

Moreover the way in which Khrushchev argued is an abdication of political realism. It may or may not be true that any particular feeling exists anywhere: but to rule it out as *a priori* impossible on scholastic grounds means that the authorities no longer felt themselves obliged to examine evidence outside their own documents. (The evidence refuting Khrushchev's view was in fact provided only a month after it was put forward, in the Tbilisi riots of March 1956.) But this sort of thinking is only too typical of the whole Soviet outlook – it is similar to the view often met with that there can be no strikes in a Communist country because the state is a workers' state and therefore the workers would have no interest in striking against it, or to the even more disquieting notion that since a Socialist state is by definition incapable of aggression, no military action it takes, of any sort whatever, can be called aggressive.

Where there is oppression ordered from outside and carried out largely by foreigners, the inevitable resistance will take national form – even though the original oppressive measures have no specific national character. This proposition, which has been largely forgotten by the Soviet leaders, seems to be the key to the enormous strength of national feeling in the Soviet bloc. The cases of Hungary and Czechoslovakia were particularly striking demonstrations of the theme.

Certainly the Soviet Government has made partial amends for the deportation decisions taken by Stalin. And, as we have seen, Stalin's action in the matter has been condemned as contrary to Leninist principles.

What this means is not so certain. It is true that Lenin laid down as a general principle that nations should be treated on a basis of equality. But, as was shown in Chapter 8, he makes it clear that in practice the interests of a given nation may be contrary to those of the world revolution, and that in that case its national interests may, and in fact must, be suppressed.

If the aspirations of a nation clash with those of the world revolution (incarnate in the government of the Soviet Union), perhaps even to the extent of looking towards independence, the case against it would be established. If such a nation were in a strategic area, the interests of the Soviet Union might well require its deportation. And in fact, in rather a different context, Khrushchev and Suslov opposed turning the Crimea into a Jewish settlement area on the grounds that *that* nation's habitation of the area would enable it to be used against the Soviet Union.

The old Communist Lozovksy, with the leading Yiddish writers of the Soviet Union, David Bergelson, Itzik Feffer and others, most of whom had been under arrest since 1949 when the Jewish anti-Fascist Committee was dissolved by the secret police, were executed on 12 August 1952 on a charge of trying to turn the Crimea into a Jewish state with the object of detaching it from the USSR.

The only basis for this charge was that there had indeed been suggestions for the restoration and extension of the Jewish settlements which had existed in the Crimea before the war. Under Khrushchev the victims of the 'Crimean Affair' were quietly rehabilitated, but Khrushchev remarked that all the same he 'agreed with Stalin that the Crimea, which at the end of the anti-Hitlerite war had become depopulated, should not become a centre of Jewish colonization, as in case of war it would have been transformed into a *place d'armes* against the Soviet Union'.[1] And the fact that the Crimea and Meskhetia are the only truly strategic areas involved in the deportations, and that they are two of the three in which it has *not* been felt necessary to permit the re-establishment of national rights, may be taken to imply that his successors have differed from Stalin not in principle but simply in holding a less strict interpretation of what areas are strategically sensitive. If this is so, it is an opinion depending on military factors which might change, and on military opinions which might vary. In that case there can be no guarantee that the stricter view might not again prevail in Soviet government circles, and further trouble ensue for unsatisfactory nations.

For, in any case, while Khrushchev condemned the policy pursued by Stalin in the matter, even he nowhere condemned in any way the structure of Soviet rule which made such a decision possible. That the governing councils of the Soviet Union sitting at the Kremlin actually decided to deport these nations is indeed reprehensible, as Khrushchev says. But it is equally reprehensible that they should be *in a position to do so at all*. It is hard to follow how it can be maintained that the nations of the USSR have any rights or powers, when these are admittedly abolished or restored by simple fiat from Moscow. Now, as before, the national minorities of the USSR depend, even for their very existence, upon policy decisions in which they have no say.

It seems probable that the main reason for the announcement of the repatriation of the deported peoples was the pressure of opinion in Free Asia. Some of the facts had become fairly widely known, and in the present period when Asian goodwill is important in Soviet foreign policy, a balance of advantage may be thought to have lain in the course now taken. That pressure of world opinion may, in such circumstances, have some effect in the USSR is a very welcome state of affairs, and the fact that some measure of relief has thus been afforded to the decimated populations is most encouraging. It cannot be concealed, however, that attention to the susceptibilities of Asians not under Soviet rule is one thing and that any genuine feeling about the rights of the nations already within the Soviet Union is another. And the only too obvious implication is that if ever *all* the Asian populations came within the Communist belt, these pressures would no longer exist and there would be no reason to expect any concessions from Moscow.

Even as it is, such pressures, and whatever other motives the Soviet leaders may have for the changes of policy, are no substitute for real guarantees of the rights of the smaller nations of the Soviet Union. 'The Soviet Government giveth and the Soviet Government taketh away. Blessed be the Soviet

Government' is not a formula that is likely to be subscribed to with any enthusiasm by local patriots.

Even on the personality level, and even if we accept Khrushchev's thesis and blame the whole business on Stalin, no constitutional changes have taken place in the USSR to prevent the emergence of another Stalin. Nor have the present rulers of the Soviet Union showed themselves to differ in principle on questions of national rights, as was shown in Hungary in November 1956 and in Czechoslovakia in August 1968. Their view of policy may tend to make them less ready to give such obvious affronts to national aspirations as Stalin did in the deportations. And, indeed, we may grant not only to Khrushchev, but even to his successors, that they wish as far as possible to act by persuasion and compromise, and keep overt terror and violence, at least, to what they would judge a necessary minimum. But this is only a comparative matter, and when Soviet interests appeared to be affected in an important way they were ready enough to act.

In any case, the fate of the subject nations continues to depend solely on decisions taken in Moscow. The great lesson of the actions taken in 1941 to 1944 and described in these pages is simply that no sanction exists to modify those decisions, even when they are to the effect that a nation's existence shall cease.

In fact, in a sense the Chinese rulers were no more than carrying accepted Communist principles to a logical conclusion when they showed themselves prepared to accept the disappearance of whole nations in nuclear war, and urged that the Communist Parties of these nations should themselves accept such a fate for the world victory of Communism:

> When a Czechoslovak journalist, in a conversation with Tao Chu, a member of the Central Committee of the CCP, pointed out that in Czechoslovakia, where 14,000,000 people live, the whole nation might perish in the event of thermonuclear war, he was given the reply: 'In the event of a destructive war the small countries of the Socialist camp will have to subordinate their interests to the general interests of

the entire camp as a whole.' Another responsible official of the Chinese Peoples' Republic, in a conversation with Soviet representatives, asserted that Comrade Togliatti, Secretary-General of the Italian Communist Party, was wrong when he expressed concern for the fate of his people and said that in the event of thermonuclear war all Italy would be destroyed. 'But other peoples will remain,' said this official, 'and imperialism will be annihilated.'[2]

This comes, indeed, from a partisan source – from the Russian. Still, it is certainly in accord with Nehru's conversation with Mao Tse-tung, when the latter said that in a world war, even if half the population were destroyed, socialism would be victorious, and soon make up the deficit.[3]

This sort of logic does not have much appeal when openly expressed; and it is doubtless not easy for less purely fanatical figures to accept it. We should not assume even of Communism that all doctrines are always liable to be taken to their logical conclusions. All the same, the subordination of national rights, and even of national existence, to the interests of the regime as a whole, is and always has been a basic Communist principle.

The Soviet invasion of Czechoslovakia is also highly relevant. The doctrine of 'limited sovereignty' announced by Moscow to justify it is wholly in accord with the doctrines examined in Chapter 8. *Pravda*, on 26 September 1968, said that nations do have the right to decide their own development, but added that 'none of their decisions, however, must harm socialism in their country, the basic interests of other socialist countries or the whole world workers' movement', adding that 'World socialism ... is indivisible.' Andrei Gromyko, the Soviet Foreign Minister, said much the same at the UN on 3 October, speaking of 'the inviolable frontiers of the Socialist Commonwealth'. Soviet Vice-Premier K. Mazurov quoted a declaration of the 1960 Conference of Communist Parties, to the effect that each ruling Communist Party 'bears a historical responsibility for the fate both of its own country and for the whole socialist commonwealth'. Finally, Leonid Brezhnev himself announced at the 5th Congress of the Polish United Workers Party in

Warsaw on 12 November 1968 that 'any threat to the cause of socialism within a socialist country' becomes not only a problem for the people of a given country 'but also the joint problem and the concern of all socialist countries'.

It will be seen that all this is precisely in accord with Stalin's theme that 'Apart from the right of nations to self-determination, there is the right of the working class to consolidate its power and to this latter right the right of self-determination is subordinate.' The Czechoslovaks and the Crimeans are faced with an identical claim – that the interests and desires of the Politburo in Moscow must have precedence over theirs.

And as to the personal records, as well as the political convictions, of some of the present leaders, General Peter Grigorenko was being understandably pessimistic when, in his speech of 17 March 1968, he warned the Crimean Tatars: 'You think you have only to deal with honest people. This is not the case. What was done to your nation was not done by Stalin alone. And his accomplices are not only alive but holding responsible offices.'

14

THE CRIMEAN
CONFRONTATION

THE rehabilitation of the Crimean Tatars in September 1967 was not to be the end of the story. The period since then has seen a struggle by the Tatars to regain the right still denied them of returning to their ancestral homeland. And this struggle has not only received unprecedented public support from the group of Moscow intellectuals who demand from the Brezhnev regime a general policy of liberalization, but it has also been widely and effectively reported in the West as well. Probably more people are now aware of the predicament of the Tatars than at any time in the whole period of the anti-national activities of the Stalin and post-Stalin regimes.

While the question of rehabilitating the Crimean Tatars was being considered, but before the decree had been promulgated, their representatives were received on 21 July 1967 by the Secretary of the Presidium of the Supreme Soviet, Georgadze; the head of the KGB, Andropov; the Minister of Public Order, Shchelokov; and the Prosecutor-General, Rudenko. They were told that the question was a matter solely for the authorities. Andropov is said to have added, in the name of the Politburo, that the problem was still on their agenda, and that the political rehabilitation of the Crimean Tatars was not necessarily the last word. Their movement was understandable, and could continue, but only if they expressed it in a legal fashion. There is some hint here that the continued exclusion of the Tatars from their homeland involved a political debit which the Polit-buro were not sure was worth it – and here lie the seeds of future hope. But the Tatars were henceforth continually faced with arguments about the Soviet *raison d'état* in the Crimea. Andropov's formulation was soon interpreted to mean that any attempt to dispute the official view was 'anti-Soviet'. And the authors of documents claiming Tatar rights were arrested and tried.

In a 'letter-statement' addressed to the Central Committee and to the Supreme Soviet[1] the Crimean Tatar representatives complained that the Decree of 5 September 1967 in effect sanctioned their forcible transfer to Uzbekistan and other republics; and they again called for what had been denied them, the right to return to their motherland, the Crimea. Tatars attempting to return to the Crimea in 1967 were, the letter went on, kept out by physical force, while complaints made about this had no effect. Attempts had been made to break up Tatar solidarity by agents provocateurs. Those who wished to return to the Crimea were decried as 'autonomists' and 'adventurists'; and they were called on to accept their 'reservations' in Uzbekistan. The local authorities had tried to suppress the movement 'like the Memphis racists'. The letter pointed out that there was still continual emigration from the Ukraine to the Crimea, so clearly the argument that the country was full and could not admit its old inhabitants was false. It ended up with the sad remark that in case the petition were refused the Tatars would have no recourse but to employ their right to turn to the international organizations in Human Rights Year.

A series of arrests and trials culminated on 21 April 1968, when the Crimean Tatars at Chirchik in Uzbekistan held on Lenin's birthday a national and cultural meeting with singing and dancing. They were attacked by the local police with high-pressure hoses and truncheons.

Those directly responsible for the Chirchik repressions are named by the Crimeans as the Secretary of the City Committee of the Party, Yakubov, and Major-General Sharaliev, commanding the local troops, both of whom had personally threatened the Tatar leaders, while the Russian Secretary of the Uzbek Communist Party, Lomonosov, is held directly to blame for the 'Black Hundred' methods employed. (The Samarkand local authorities too had, it was complained, instigated racial trouble in their city, among other things spreading rumours that the Crimean Tatars had desecrated an Armenian cemetery – a typical Tsarist manœuvre.)

About 300 of the Chirchik demonstrators were arrested, apparently on the grounds that they had resisted authority. However, only twelve, the majority of whom had not been present at the meeting, were proceeded against, for 'breaches of public order', receiving sentences of from six months to two and a half years in labour camp. Ayder Bariev, a Tatar tractor driver, flew to Moscow to protest and on 22 April sent a telegram of protest to the Prosecutor-General, Rudenko. The latter however made no reply to telegrams and letters from Bariev and a group of Crimean Tatar representatives which followed him to Moscow, refused to receive them and made no inquiry into their complaints.

Following this up, a letter to the Prosecutor from one of the best known of the intellectual protesters in Moscow, General Grigorenko, who had become deeply concerned with their case, laid out in full the complaint of the Crimean Tatars at their maltreatment in Chirchik and afterwards. Grigorenko pointed out that among Rudenko's constitutional duties is that of checking on police illegality, and that far from fulfilling this duty the Prosecutor's office was not even prepared to receive the complaints at all.[2]

Eight hundred Crimean Tatars who had come to present petitions were expelled from Moscow in the summer of 1968. The Moscow Assistant Prosecutor Stasenkov told them that the Tatar question had been decided 'fully and finally' and that there would be no more concessions. A group of them were arrested actually in the building of the Central Committee, together with some Russian sympathizers. The whole operation was managed by General Volkov, head of the Moscow branch of the MOOP (formerly, and now again, MVD). They were rounded up everywhere and sent under guard in a baggage train to Tashkent.

So on 21 July 1968 the Crimean Tatars issued their appeal to 'world public opinion', setting out their demands and calling for help to bring about a return to their homeland. It was signed by 118 people, who had been selected by their local communities 'to fight by all legal means for the return to the Homeland'. The appeal revealed that since 1959 more than 200 Crimean Tatars had been sentenced to up to seven years' imprisonment 'although they have always acted within the framework of the Soviet Constitution'.

A climax in the campaign of the Soviet authorities against the Crimean movement came on 1 July 1969, when ten leading Crimeans were sent for trial in Tashkent on charges of anti-Soviet propaganda. Six of the ten were born in 1940 or later: that is, they are precisely of the 'new generation' referred to in the rehabilitation decree as having 'emerged and joined the country's labour force and political life'. One of their leaders is the physicist R. K. Kadiyev. (In 1968 he had presented to an international conference in Tbilisi a much admired paper on the relation of recent astronomical discoveries to the theory of relativity. It was warmly praised in *Za Kommunism*, 22 November 1968.) After a trial lasting a month, Kadiyev and three others were sentenced to up to three years in labour camps. The remainder got one-year sentences or less, and as they had already been under arrest for that length of time this meant immediate release.

As the trial was in preparation, the authorities had finally, on 7 May 1969, arrested General Grigorenko, who had gone to Tashkent to support the accused. Other arrests of Moscow liberals followed.

Fifty-five leading Moscow figures still at large (notably Peter Yakir, historian and son of the General Yakir murdered by Stalin, and himself a veteran of the labour camps) sent on 22 May 1969 an appeal with 55 signatures to the United Nations Commission on Human Rights. In this it is made clear that the Crimean question has long since become recognized as part and parcel of the whole political struggle for civil liberty now going on in the USSR.

But it is also worth emphasizing that, even in the context of national rights alone, treatment of the Crimeans is no more than an extreme example of a general policy of the Soviet Government towards the minorities. And at the same time the resentment and resistance of the Crimeans, right up to the present, can be taken as no more than a particularly strong, but otherwise not untypical, minority reaction. The solidarity of the minority nations, and the attacks on nationalist feeling, are both omnipresent in the peripheral republics of the USSR. The writer Alexei Kosterin, who joined the Bolsheviks in 1916, in his letter to the Politburo dated 24 October 1968, returning his Party card, mentioned that he had been temporarily expelled from the Party in 1958 for defending the Chechens. Having already been in trouble for defending the Volga Germans, he was now being accused of having come to the defence of the Crimean Tatars. At his funeral on 14 November 1968, a number of Crimean Tatars spoke. Some Volga Germans also attended, but the text produced by General Grigorenko remarks that their situation was worse even than that of the Tatars, so that their names could not be given. A Chechen writer and Party member, Khalid Oshayev, also spoke strongly in favour of restoring the Crimean Republic.[3] And, as we have seen, the Meskhetian movement, devoted to parallel aims, has remained active and unsatisfied.

On the wider stage the Ukrainians now demanding their own rights have also expressed solidarity with the Crimeans – even though it is to the Ukraine that the Crimeans have lost their land. (It is similarly striking that while Ukrainian nationalism had long a reputation of being anti-Semitic as well as anti-Russian, its latest manifestation strongly emphasized solidarity with the Jewish population which the Ukrainians rightly see as also suffering from various oppressive acts.)

The first signs of the present wave of trouble in the Ukraine arose in 1962–3 when Khrushchev was putting into force the new emphasis on Moscow centralism throughout the Soviet Union. A still unexplained incident in March 1964 brought feeling to a head – the burning of a section of the national library in Kiev, containing Ukrainian literature. It was commonly believed in Ukrainian circles that KGB agents, wishing to cause trouble, were responsible. (There had been similar burnings in the national libraries of Central Asian republics.) In the Ukrainian case, the culprit was caught and received what struck everyone as a very light sentence. In circumstances like these, unproved suspicions gain wide credence. It is certainly true that this was just the time when the KGB was performing acts of political provocation on its own initiative, such as the mustard gassing of a West German Embassy technician. Politically, the point is that many people felt that the KGB and the factions associated with it, whether directly responsible or not, represented the same political attitudes as the arsonist.

During this period the monument to the national poet Shevchenko became, like the Mayakovsky statue in Moscow, a rallying-point at which heterodox poetry was read, including forbidden poems of Shevchenko himself. Then various arrests followed through 1965–6 and the trials which ensued had one extraordinary result. A representative of Ukrainian television present, Chornovil, was much shocked and expressed this in protests culminating in a long denunciation of police practice addressed to the KGB. He was then himself arrested. And a series of other trials followed, accompanied by such protests as the 'Letter of 139' in 1968. Ukrainian resistance was quite closely connected with the general intellectual rebellion in Moscow. But it seems to have been on a much broader scale, and to have involved members of the Party apparatus itself, and its tone was unmistakably national.

It is clear, too, from Soviet and other reports that national feeling is also powerful in the Baltic States. In the Latvian capital, Riga, Ivan Yakhimovich, one of the dissident Soviet intellectuals, in a last letter before his arrest, appealed to Latvians not to forget that there are thousands of their countrymen in the labour camps of Mordovia and Siberia. Recent attacks on nationalist moods in Lithuania, where they are 'particularly tenacious',[4] and in Estonia, where a group of scientists has demanded national and social liberty, point to the same picture.

Even more important are signs that the struggle of the Crimean Tatars is watched with particular interest and sympathy by the other and far larger Turkic nations of the USSR. And all this diverse yet interlocking resistance gains even greater significance when we consider that the 1970 census is expected to show, for the first time, the Russian people in a minority in the USSR.

In the post-war world, one of the most insistent problems that has faced the advanced countries has been the demands for independence on the part of peoples previously ruled from the metropolitan centres. Moscow can surely no more escape this confrontation (as opposed to delaying it by sheer force) than it can the other problems facing a modern state. At present the Crimean Tatars are a test case. In the broader sense they always have been.

We can be certain that recent publicity for the Crimeans in the West has been to the good. When the decisions of the rulers are governed by the balance of political advantage, the more they are shown a debit in their international reputation, and in trouble at home, the more they are likely to feel the balance tilt against the 'strategic' *raison d'état*. At any rate, that seems the best prospect for the Crimean Tatars in obtaining at least the amount of justice involved in letting them return to their homes.

Meanwhile, the present authorities in Moscow are in any case committed to complete centralism as far as actual power and policies are concerned. The changes in attitude to the minority nations can only be seen as tactical ones, within those limitations. Sometimes more, sometimes less, concession is made to local feeling in an effort to secure as far as possible the acceptance of inessential concessions to national feeling as a substitute for the essential.

Yet here, as in other spheres, Soviet authorities find themselves caught in a contradiction. To take a single instance: the reviling of local national heroes like Shamil and the insistence on obeisance to all things Russian produces resentment. On the other hand admitting that Shamil was a heroic figure and allowing this to be taught in the local schools encourages national sentiment, and in a form which can hardly fail to be anti-Russian. The present compromise on this particular issue, whereby both sides are right, is a forced and unreal one and is likely to make the worst of both worlds.

In almost all spheres, indeed, the choice that seems to present itself to the Communist rulers is between oppression and relaxation. The experience of the past few years has shown that repression produces troubles which can apparently only be coped with by relaxation, but that relaxation then produces troubles which require repression. This is an old problem in autocracies, and one which has never been satisfactorily solved.

Enormously important though the national question is in itself, the principles applied in it may in this sense too be regarded as typical of the entire range of Soviet political, social and cultural action. In any case, the more widely the facts become known in the West, especially in those cases where they have long been concealed or distorted, the more real our picture of the world will be.

APPENDIX 1

CHRONOLOGY

28 Aug.	1941	Decree on the deportation of the Volga Germans.
7 Sept.	1941	Decree on the partition of the former Volga-German Republic.
Oct.–Nov.	1943	Deportation of the Karachai.
December	1943	Deportation of the Kalmyks.
27 Dec.	1943	Decree on the deportation of the Kalmyks and setting up of the Astrakhan Province.
22 Feb.	1944	Deportation of the Chechens and Ingushi.
7 Mar.	1944	Decree on the deportation of the Chechens and Ingushi.
9 Mar.	1944	Award of Order of Suvorov 1st Class to Serov.
22 Mar.	1944	Setting up of the Grozny Province.
Mar.–Apr.	1944	Deportation of the Balkars.
18–19 May	1944	Deportation of the Crimean Tatars.
30 June	1944	Decree transforming the Crimean Republic into the Crimean Province.
15 Nov.	1944	Deportation of the Meskhetians.
26 June	1946	Publication of decree on the deportation of the Chechens, Ingushi and Crimean Tatars.
10 Feb.	1948	Central Committee pronouncement on music, attacking the Chechens and Ingushi.
May	1950	Denunciation of Shamil.
August	1952	Secret trial of Jews in the 'Crimean Affair'.
19 Feb.	1954	Decree transferring the Crimea from the RSFSR to the Ukraine.

14 Mar.	1955	Decree transferring Karachai territory from Georgia to the RSFSR.
17 May	1955	First mention of Chechens in exile.
	1955	Unpublished decrees releasing deported peoples from direct NKVD control.
January	1956	First attempts to rehabilitate Shamil.
24–5 Feb.	1956	Khrushchev's Secret Speech.
9 Jan.	1957	Decrees of the Presidium of the Supreme Soviet on restoring the national autonomy of the Balkars, Chechens, Ingushi, Kalmyks and Karachai.
11 Jan.	1957	Decree of the Presidium of the Supreme Soviet on transfer of Chechen territory from Georgia to the RSFSR.
11 Feb.	1957	Law of the Supreme Soviet confirming decrees of 9 January and 11 January.
March	1957	Official repudiation of rehabilitators of Shamil and imposition of a moderate Stalinist view.
29 July	1958	Decree transforming the Kalmyk Autonomous Province into the Kalmyk ASSR.
end of	1958	Date for the completion of the return of the Kalmyks, Karachai and Balkars.
end of	1960	Date for the completion of the return of the Chechens and Ingushi.
October	1961	Adoption of present Party programme.
29 Aug.	1964	Decree of the Presidium of the Supreme Soviet on the rehabilitation of the Volga Germans.
5 Sept.	1967	Decree of the Presidium of the Supreme Soviet on the rehabilitation of the Crimean Tatars.
30 May	1968	Decree of the Presidium of the Supreme Soviet on the Meskhetians.
1 July–5 Aug.	1969	Tashkent Trial.

APPENDIX 2

THE UNITED NATIONS
GENOCIDE CONVENTION

A 'Convention on the Prevention and Punishment of the Crime of Genocide' was adopted by the United Nations General Assembly on 9 December 1948. It came into effect in 1950 and was ratified by the USSR in 1954. The substantive articles are as follows:

Article I

The contracting parties confirm that genocide, whether committed in time of peace or in time of war, is a crime under international law which they undertake to prevent and punish.

Article II

In the present Convention genocide means any of the following acts committed with intent to destroy, in whole or in part, a national, ethnical, racial or religious group, as such:

(*a*) Killing members of the group;

(*b*) Causing grievous bodily or mental harm to members of the group;

(*c*) Deliberately inflicting on the group conditions of life calculated to bring about its physical destruction in whole or in part;

(*d*) Imposing measures intended to prevent births within the group;

(*e*) Forcibly transferring children of the group to another group.

The second edition of the *Large Soviet Encyclopaedia* has an article on the subject in which it describes genocide as 'an offshoot of decaying imperialism'.

NOTES

Chapter 1: THE RUSSIANS MOVE SOUTH
1. A. P. Berzhe, *Chechniya and the Chechens* (Tiflis, 1859).

Chapter 2: IN THE MOUNTAINS
1. Stalin, *Marxism and the National and Colonial Question*, English edition (London, 1947), p. 104.
2. *Collection of Decrees and Regulations of the Workers' and Peasants' Government*, No. 2 (1917), Article 18.
3. *Collection of Decrees and Regulations of the Workers' and Peasants' Government*, No. 6 (19 December 1917), Appendix 2e.
4. Stalin, *Works*, English edition (Moscow, 1953, etc.), vol. IV, p. 415.
5. I. Borisenko, *Soviet Republics in the North Caucasus in 1918* (Rostov, 1930), vol. II, pp. 72–3.
6. Stalin, *Works*, vol. IV, p. 415.
7. *Revolutsiya i Natsionalnosti*, No. 7 (1930), pp. 23–4.
8. *Revolutsiya i Natsionalnosti*, No. 12 (1935), pp. 66–7.
9. *Revolutsiya i Natsionalnosti*, No. 72 (November 1931).
10. *Revolutsiya i Natsionalnosti*, No. 50 (April 1934).
11. *Report of the Court Proceedings in the Case of the Anti-Soviet Bloc of Rights and Trotskyites*, English edition (Moscow, 1938), pp. 118–21.
12. Ibid., pp. 164–6.
13. *Soviet War News* (6 October 1942).
14. E. Genkina, *The Formation of the U.S.S.R.* (Moscow, 1943).
15. *Khronika*, No. 7 (1969).

Chapter 3: STEPPE, PENINSULA AND VOLGA
1. W. K. Matthews, *Languages of the U.S.S.R.* (Cambridge, 1951).
2. *Collection of Decrees and Regulations of the Workers' and Peasants' Government*, No. 37, Article 368.
3. *Soviet War News* (9 February 1943).
4. *Poetry of Kalmykia* (Moscow, 1940).
5. *Literaturnaya Gazeta* (27 May 1952).
6. *Sovietskaya Kirgizia* (23 March 1956).
7. *Revolutsiya i Natsionalnosti*, No. 12 (1935), pp. 66–7.
8. *Bulletin of the Supreme Soviet*, No. 40 (1941): quoted in *Collection of Laws of the Soviet Union and Decrees of the Presidium of the Supreme Soviet 1938–1958* (Moscow, 1958).

Chapter 4: HOW MANY WENT?
1. Walter Kolarz, *Russia and Her Colonies* (London, 1953), p. 75.

Chapter 5: THE MEMORY HOLE
1. Kolarz, op. cit., p. 75.
2. *Voprosy Istorii*, No. 12 (1948).
3. 4 June 1952.
4. *Pravda* (11 February 1948).
5. I. M. Razgon, *Ordzhonikidze and Kirov in the Struggle for the Soviet Regime in the North Caucasus* (Moscow, 1941).
6. A. A. Askerov and others, *Soviet State Law* (Moscow, 1948).
7. Evtikhiev & Vlasov, *Administrative Law of the U.S.S.R.* (Moscow, 1946), p. 324.

Chapter 6: THE TRIAL OF SHAMIL
1. E. Genkina, *Formation of the U.S.S.R.* (Moscow, 1943), p. 76.
2. Vol. XI (Moscow, 1947).
3. E.g. *Voprosy Istorii*, No. 11 (1947).
4. *Bakinsky Rabochii* (30 November 1961).
5. *Journal of the U.S.S.R. Academy of Sciences, Division of Literature and Language*, No. 3 (December 1950).
6. *Voprosy Istorii*, No. 10 (October, 1950).
7. No. 6 (November–December 1950).
8. E.g., N. A. Smirnov, *Studies in the History of the Study of Islam in the U.S.S.R.* (Moscow, 1954); S. K. Bushuev, *From the History of Foreign Political Relations at the Time of the Unification of the Caucasus and Russia* (Moscow, 1954); A. V. Fadeev, in *Voprosy Istorii*, No. 6 (1955).

Chapter 7: BEHIND THE SOVIET SILENCE
1. A. Avtorkhanov, *Narodoubiystvo v SSSR* (Munich, 1952). Avtorkhanov's work on Chechen history, *On the Basic Problems of the History of Chechniya*, is cited as a source in the *Large Soviet Encyclopaedia* (First Edition), and is even referred to, though without the author's name, in a post-war collection, *Musical Culture of the Autonomous Republics of the RSFSR*.
2. Alexander Uralov, *The Reign of Stalin* (London, 1953).
3. *Sotsialisticheskiy Vestnik*, No. 3 (March 1951).
4. There is an interesting account from the German side in *Wenn Sie Verderben Wollen*, Jürgen Thorwald (Stuttgart, 1952).
5. Ivan Kozlov, *In the Crimean Underground* (Moscow, 1947).
6. See *Life* (5 July 1954); Simon Wolin and Robert M. Slusser, *The Soviet Secret Police* (New York, 1957), pp. 324–6.
7. Kolarz, op. cit., p. 193.
8. The Calcutta *Statesman*, 4 May 1955.
9. *Znamya*, No. 9 (1963).
10. Antoni Ekart, *Vanished without Trace* (London, 1954), p. 222.
11. Ralph Jones, 'Climbing with the Russians', *Geographical Magazine* (June 1959).
12. Wolfgang Leonhard, *Child of the Revolution* (London, 1957).

13. Alexander Solzhenitsyn, *The Cancer Ward*, vol. I, chap. 19.
14. *Khronika*, No. 7 (1969).
15. Vol. XII, passed for press 28 May 1952.

Chapter 8: COMMUNISM AND THE NATIONAL QUESTION

1. Stalin, 1913, *Marxism and the National and Colonial Question*, p. 13.
2. Lenin, *Selected Works*, English edition (London, 1935, etc.), vol. IV, p. 250.
3. Lenin, 1916, *Selected Works*, vol. V, p. 270.
4. Lenin, *Selected Works*, vol. XI, p. 352.
5. Lenin, 1914, *Sochineniya*, 4th ed. (Moscow, 1941, etc.), vol. 20, p. 378.
6. Lenin, 1914, *Sochineniya*, vol. 20, p. 411.
7. Lenin, 1916, *Selected Works*, vol. V, p. 305.
8. Lenin, 1916, *Sochineniya*, vol. 22, pp. 326, 330.
9. Stalin, *Works*, vol. VI, p. 147.
10. Marx, 'Democratic Panslavism', *Neue Rheinische Zeitung* (February 1849).
11. Engels, Letter to Kautsky (7 February 1882).
12. Lenin, *Sochineniya*, vol. 20, pp. 403, 406.
13. Stalin, *Problems of Leninism* (1924), p. 74.
14. Stalin, *Works*, vol. V, p. 270.
15. M. Kammari, 'Socialist Nations of the U.S.S.R. under Conditions of Transition from Socialism to Communism', *Kommunist*, No. 15 (October 1953).
16. Lenin, *Sochineniya*, vol. 26, p. 408.
17. Stalin, 1920, *Works*, vol. IV, p. 365.
18. Stalin, 1921, *Works*, vol. V, pp. 18–19.
19. Stalin, 1913, *Works*, vol. II, p. 376.
20. Lenin, *Sochineniya*, vol. 19, p. 453.
21. Stalin, *Works*, vol. XIII, pp. 32–3.
22. Letter of Stalin to Lenin of 12 June 1920. Not contained in Stalin's *Collected Works*, but found in Lenin's *Collected Works* in the unexpurgated third edition (Russian, 1932), vol. XXV, p. 624.
23. Stalin, *Marxism and the National and Colonial Question*.
24. Lenin, 1922, *Sochineniya*, 33, p. 267.
25. *Communist Party Programme* (1918).
26. *Twelfth Congress of the Russian Communist Party (Bolsheviks), Stenographic Report* (Moscow, 1923), p. 472.
27. Stalin, *Works*, vol. IV, p. 363.
28. Stalin, *Works*, vol. IV, pp. 370–1.
29. E.g. in *Kommunist* (October 1953).
30. *Large Soviet Encyclopaedia*, 1st edition, vol. VIII.
31. *Voprosy Istorii*, No. 10 (1954), p. 38.
32. *Kommunist*, No. 6 (1955), p. 79.
33. E. Genkina, *The Formation of the U.S.S.R.*, p. 3.
34. *Voprosy Istorii*, No. 9 (1957).

Chapter 9: CONSTITUTIONAL ARRANGEMENTS AND SOVIET PRACTICE

1. *The Theory of State and Law* (Moscow, 1949), p. 380.

2. M. Kalinin, *During these Years* (Moscow, 1929), vol. III, p. 385.
3. Academician E. Zhukov in the Soviet English-language magazine *News* (March 1956).
4. *Voprosy Istorii* (October 1955).
5. *Kulturnoe Stroitelstvo* (Moscow, 1958).
6. *Partiinaya Zhizn*, No. 8 (1957).
7. *Komsomolskaya Pravda* (24 April 1957).
8. *Voprosy Filosofii* (June 1963).
9. *Kommunist* (December 1962).
10. *Partiinaya Zhizn* (December 1962).
11. *Voprosy Filosofii*, No. 1 (1957).
12. Lenin, *Works*, vol. V, 31, p. 126.
13. *Kommunist*, No. 11 (1949).
14. Ts. Stepanyan in *Krasnaya Zvezda*, 29 January 1970.

Chapter 10: FIVE NATIONS REAPPEAR

1. *Kazakhstanskaya Pravda* (4 July 1956).
2. *Pravda* (12 February 1957).
3. *Bulletin of the Supreme Soviet*, No. 5 (1955), quoted in *Collection of Laws of the Soviet Union and Decrees of the Presidium of the Supreme Soviet 1938–1958*.
4. *Pravda* (12 February 1957).
5. Kolarz, op. cit., p. 177.
6. *Bulletin of the Supreme Soviet*, No. 8 (875) (20 April 1957).
7. *Caucasian Review*, No. 6, p. 151.
8. *Narodnoe Obrazovanie* (May 1957).
9. 'Brotherly Collaboration of the Peoples of the U.S.S.R.', *Aid to Political Self-Education*, No. 10 (October 1957). These figures are also printed in *Voprosy Filosofii*, No. 5 (1957).
10. *Groznenskii Rabochii* (12 January 1958).
11. *Groznenskii Rabochii* (31 January 1958).
12. *Groznenskii Rabochii* (25 March 1958).
13. *Pravda* (2 September 1958).
14. *Groznenskii Rabochii* (12 January 1958).
15. *Sovietskaya Rossiya* (26 August 1962).
16. *Sovietskaya Rossiya* (11 October 1962).
17. *Partiinaya Zhizn*, No. 6 (March 1966).
18. Letter No. 7/3 from the First Department of the Uzbek MOOP to Major-General Kiselev, Chairman of the Uzbek KGB: quoted in General Grigorenko's letter of 10 March 1969. See *Posev*, No. 6 (1969).
19. Letter No. 7/8–2026 (5 February 1968), quoted as above.

Chapter 11: SOME FURTHER REWRITING

1. *Voprosy Istorii*, No. 2 (1956). (For a fuller discussion of this controversy, see Lowell Tillett's *The Great Friendship* (Chapel Hill, 1969) pp. 199–222, 262–9.)
2. Ibid. No. 3 (1956).
3. Ibid. No. 2 (1956).
4. Ibid. No. 12 (1956).

5. Ibid. No. 12 (1956).
6. *Novy Mir*, No. 9 (1967).
7. *The Musical Culture of the Autonomous Republics of the R.S.F.S.R.*, ed. G. I. Litinsky (Moscow, 1957).

Chapter 12: NATIONS STILL IN EXILE

1. *Osteuropa-Recht*, No. 1 (July 1958). Quoting *The Bulletin of Current Legislation of the U.S.S.R.*, No. 5 (December 1955).
2. *Sovietskaya Kirgizia* (25 July 1963).
3. *Bulletin of the Supreme Soviet*, No. 52 (28 December 1964).
4. *Bulletin of the Supreme Soviet*, No. 36 (8 September 1967).
5. *Yazyki Narodov S.S.S.R.*, vol. II (Moscow, 1966).
6. *Khronika*, No. 7 (1969).
7. *Bulletin of the Supreme Soviet of the U.S.S.R.*, No. 23 (5 June 1968).
8. For the Meskhetians see especially *Khronika*, No. 7 and No. 9 (*Posev*, 2nd Special Number, December 1969).

Chapter 13: RESPONSIBILITIES

1. *Morgen Freiheit* (12 December 1956).
2. Suslov's report to the Plenum of the C.C. CPSU (14 February 1962), *Pravda* (3 April 1964).
3. New China News Agency, 31 August 1963; and see Edgar Snow, in *Sunday Times*, 14 February 1965; Chen Yi in *L'Express*, 26 October–1 November 1964.

Chapter 14: THE CRIMEAN CONFRONTATION

1. *Novoe Russkoe Slovo* (5 October 1968); and see for other recent documents on the Crimean movement *Novoe Russkoye Slovo*, 28 March 1969; *Novy Zhurnal*, No. 97 (December 1969); *Survey*, No. 72 (1969).
2. *Posev* (January 1969).
3. *Posev*, No. 4 (1969).
4. *Pravda* (24 January 1969).

INDEX